Third Enlarged Edition

Arubafirina

The Book of Fairy Magic

Almine

Plus: Secrets of the Hidden Kingdoms

Published by Spiritual Journeys LLC

First Edition May 1, 2007
Second Edition June 16, 2009
Third Edition June 6, 2011

Copyright 2006
MAB 998 Megatrust

By Almine
Spritual Journeys LLC
P.O. Box 300
Newport, Oregon 97365

www.spiritualjourneys.com
877-552-5646

Cover Illustration—Charles Frizzell
Fairy Sketches—Judy Uchikura
Text Design—Stacey Freibert
Layout—Ariel Frailich

Manufactured in the United States of America

ISBN: 978-1-936926-32-9 Softcover

ISBN: 978-1-936926-33-6 Adobe Reader

Table of Contents

Appendices

Dedication

This book is dedicated to the fairies, elves, and other magical beings of the fairy realms that returned to Earth from Lyra, Venus, the Pleiades, Andromeda, and Arcturus in October and November of 2006.

May the joy of your presence be uplifting to all.

Preface

As a Toltec Nagual, Almine is dedicated to a life of impeccability and of setting others free from illusion. Whereas other way-showers gather more and more students, she assists in creating more and more masters, freely sharing her vast knowledge. She has achieved the ultimate goal of the Nagual, namely, to conquer death.

The deep compassion this Immortal Master has for all life can be felt in her presence. Her writing and speaking are done from complete silence of the mind, accessed directly from Source. Because of this, she is a conduit for endless information, limited only by our willingness and ability to receive.

Foreword

From the Mother Herself, the command was given:
"Prepare yourself for that which must be written."

Holy and pure this gift from her hand,
Fairy Magic for humans to understand.

"The window will open up for but one week.
In seven days the book must complete.

On the thirteenth of November you must begin.
For seven days the knowledge will pour in.

Before it, not even the drawings will come.
As it is given, it must be done.

Even the price I give unto you.
To deter all but those whose hearts are true.

For they shall know the truth herein:
Shall sense the power for good that lies within.

Not from the Earth this knowledge comes:
But from far-flung constellations.

Hundreds of thousands of fairies from there,
Have come to Earth this knowledge to share."

"If this book is in yours hands, you are one of those
Who has been chosen this magic to know.

'Why,' may you ask, 'has this been given?'
To restore the balance, to make all even.

Fairy, faun and elf delight,
In the ending of a dark and faithless night.

The long night is over, the dawn has begun;
On the Earth, the Goddess has come"

Book I

Part One

Introduction to the Magic of the Fairy Realms

First Ring Vs. Second Ring Magic

In speaking of the magic kingdoms, it is necessary to lift the veil from magic and its uses. Magic is the manipulation of reality through the use of intent. There are two ways to practice magic: first and second ring magic.

On the walls of ancient Central American ruins, the story is told of how first ring magic was initially brought to Earth by star-beings from Orion. This form of magic is left-brain based and utilizes external techniques for its effectiveness. When most speak or think of magic, it is usually first ring magic they refer to.

Second ring magic uses the right-brain, feminine, non-cognitive methods of affecting reality. The magic originates from within rather than from without. It is inner abilities that are used by the unseen realms on Earth.

Among the kingdoms and realms on Earth, only the physical ones have forgotten their heritage as magical beings of the cosmos. As a result, their ability to do second ring magic became obscured and man resorted to the left-brain, or first ring magic.

Only in the deepest recesses of mystery schools did pockets of knowledge survive of an inner technology that could influence the environment in mystical ways. Only there were remnants taught of the knowledge that once flourished in ancient Mu and some of the older Atlantean civilizations.

The advent of first ring magic wrought havoc among men. Climates were disrupted, global catastrophes occurred and men became power-seekers and turned upon each other. The oral traditions of the Toltec seers speak of these times of great destruction when first ring magic was used in the warfare that destroyed and ravaged Atlantis.

Between 200,000 and 75,000 years ago when Atlantis was divided into two large islands, Ruta and Itiya, practitioners of first ring magic congregated on Ruta and grew strong.

Those practicing second ring magic lived on Itiya, laboring diligently to keep the Earth from experiencing another global catastrophe. At the end of the period, however, it became abundantly clear they were losing the battle. They fled to safer areas, including the Inner Earth.

The only way to obtain power without damaging the inter-connectedness of life is through perception. First ring magic uses ritual, incantations and other external sources of power. This must eventually deplete not only the practitioner, but the environment. In addition, the power available through left-brain methods is limited, whereas that available through the right-brain, internal methods is not.

First ring magic causes environmental disruption and catastrophe through depleting the environment and disrupting the Earth's energetic flow. The planetary energy flows along its ley lines, or meridians. In addition, each species has a grid telling it how to act. These grids are arrays of lines along which light in the form of information flows. When these, as well as the ley lines, are disrupted, the planet tilts on her axis or draws in other catastrophes due to lack of life force.

The potential for abuse of magic is a very real threat when first ring magic is used, since it doesn't require that the practitioner develop impeccability. Knowledge of certain practices is all that is needed. Power seekers have disrupted the environment with first ring magic since its introduction to humanity.

Second ring magic, on the other hand, is the result of perception. In fact, the more inclusive the perception the more power is available. Practitioners, because of their perception, become unable to harm life.

For the most part, the magical kingdoms have very strict rules governing the use of magic, with dire consequences for its misuse. Exceptions have been, among others, the demons and sometimes the dragons. Since the planetary and cosmic ascension began, the Mother Goddess has decreed that power to do magic be matched by a corresponding degree of perception. This removed the destructive magical abilities from beings in the cosmos.

Second ring magic has been used by fairies, elves, pixies and other beings from the magical kingdoms to create, grow and sustain plant and mineral life.[1] Angels have done the same for human and animal life. Large planetary angels sustain planets; smaller ones govern oceans, rivers, lakes and mountain ranges. Angels support humans in many ways, some staying with a single human all his life, much as a guardian spirit would.

Therefore it can be said that magic, or the power of intent, is the primary force that carries out the will of the Infinite within the cosmos. Only when it becomes exclusive or self-centered does it destroy rather than sustain life.

---

1 As described in *The Ring of Truth*, with the great changes that have taken place as a result of our ascension in August 2006, the fairy realms have moved into the direction of the East, taking on new and elevated roles in the cosmos.

The Fairies of Earth

WHY WE CAN'T SEE FAIRIES

Throughout diverse cultures, fairy tales and folk legends can be accessed at two different levels; either as entertaining tales with a moral message, or well-disguised, deep esoteric truths revealing secrets about the human psyche or the hidden realms.

One puzzling factor has always caught the attention of students of folk stories. Amongst the great variety of cultures, similarities in the details keep surfacing. Dragons breathe fire, whether in the folk tales of Peru or China. Unicorns are beneficial and healing in their interactions with man. Fairies fly and have great magical power; elves continue to delight and bring whimsy and humor to life.

Not only have these tales come from a far distant past before consciousness fell with each successive global cataclysm, but also from times when mankind as a whole could not read or write. Among the Mayans and other indigenous peoples, some sages or rulers strenuously resisted writing among their people. They knew that words or symbols would lull man into thinking he knew something because he'd named it. With a word or symbol representing an object such as a specific flower, its essence was no longer felt through the heart. In other words, that real world lying beyond form was no longer accessed.

In this way, the non-cognitive information of the universe around him became unavailable as man slowly sank into a world of logic and reason. With this shift, nine-tenths of his reality disappeared as he lost the right-brain oriented tools to discern and communicate with it. Fairies, pixies, unicorns and the other beings of the magic kingdoms, without whom the Earth would not flourish, became relegated to the realms of myth and fiction. As centuries passed, they continued to fade ever further across the horizon of human perception.

But because we have changed, doesn't mean they have ceased to be. As awareness on the planet rises to the levels from which it sank, more and more of us are once again able to communicate with the beings of these magic kingdoms, finding them delighted to befriend and aid us.

How to Cultivate Magic
From the Fairies behind Niagara Falls

A TABLETS FROM
THE STONE BOOKS LIBRARY
IN THE PIENINY MOUNTAINS, POLAND

THE MESSAGE OF STONE BOOK I

Behind the waterfall[2] under the stone
Waits a book of how to do magic for pure eyes alone
Enter with laughter and you may remain
But return to your childhood yet again
With the heart of a child you were given before[3]

2 Niagara Falls
3 Humans received magical codes in 2007

The 24 Fairy Secrets of Re-learning How to Do White Magic

1. Find a singing tree and hear its tones. Sit in silence against its trunk. Listen to the song, though not with your ears. When you hear it, your cells will start to dance. When you do this often, the magic will come.

The Greeting the Fairies Use for a Tree

Piki Pa Pahu

Note: They recommend trees that look like tuning forks.

2. Walk barefoot in the dew to clear neural pathways[4]. The reflexology points on the bottom of the feet are affected by the dew. (I asked them how.) "The dew drops tickle the blades of grass and their laughter ripples through the dew. That's why dew is so special. It's good for cuts too, so the injured area can feel good again."

---

4 Old Swiss folk remedies suggest this also

3. Create a fairy circle and say these words:

   Paalik biliblat hispiva nesut.

   Make it of flowers, shells and the feathers of birds. Sit in it and listen when the moon is full. Hear our bells and songs we'll sing for you.

4. Learn to listen with your skin. Feel the vibrations like music within. Feel the notes stroke you and listen within. The use of omni-present senses is where magic begins.

5. Practice refining your sense of smell. Then the energy[5] will rise up the spine as well. The codes of magic in the spine lie. Thus smell awakens the energy that at the base of the spine hides.

6. Find a clear stream and on its bank lie. Listen to it talk as you close your eyes. Not with its voice does it talk to you but imagine the stream is flowing through you. See where it's been as it flowed on its way. Become the stream to know what it'll say.

5 Kundalini

The Tuning Fork Tree

PHOTO TAKEN BY THE MASTER HELENA

Figure 1

7. As the hawk, so too you can fly, effortlessly soaring through the sky. Become the hawk, let your spirit be free. Practice it often until you can feel the wind through your feathers, until the Earth below you can see.

8. Magic is through joy and abundant delight, strengthened within the cord of the spine. Make a list of what brings you pleasure, incorporate it in your life to the fullest measure. Incorporate the giving of joy to yourself each day that you live, for the rest of your life.

9. To bring joy to others creates a flow that strengthens your magic. This you must know. Find ways to surprise them, let your smiles and gifts be passed on. Make the world a better place and you will be aligned with the spirit of incorruptible white magic at last.

10. Man feels alienated from the other kingdoms on Earth. It is time for his oneness with nature to be re-birthed. Lie on the Earth until you feel Her speak. A sentient being is She – get to know her as a friend.

11. The wind feels the hearts of the people in the street. It tells of their feelings to the forest's trees. The trees sing a song that helps people feel glad. Talk to the wind whenever you're sad. Speak too of wisdom that comes from your heart, of joyful celebration and songs of praise. This it will share with others as well.

12. Stones sing songs and if you ask they will show where to find what you seek, which way to go. Some stones will tell you, when among them you roam, to take them with you when you go home. Get to know them, for allies they are, to help with white magic you wish to wield.

13. From stars you can draw[6] certain qualities they have. To know how they can assist, a relationship you must form. Just like the Earth, they are sentient beings. Telepathic / empathic communication knows no distance. Instantly you will hear them like a thought within your thoughts.

6 See www.astrologyofisis.com

14. The night-time makes magic. The moon is a friend. The sharp light from the sun interferes with intent, as do the thought-forms of others. Alone in the night, when no others are near, is the best time for magic.

15. Why do fairy folk, elfin creatures, dragons, mer people and others as well, like gemstones so much? Special powers they have, some very strong. Wear them for magic – they focus intent. Angels help gemstones and you can call on them for this. Special angels we give you that help create a response when you call on gemstones to assist in white magic.

16. Start to mix potions when the moon is full. Sing their incantations, rather than just saying the words. A simple melody – just a few notes will suffice – and your potion will be stronger by far.

17. When at first you awaken the magic in you, listen as we tell you what to do. Gold is too powerful and overrides intent. Do not wear it when magic is new to you.

18. Dew has unseen properties that few can see. It rearranges old patterns that used to be. Wise ones have used it in ages gone by to erase wrinkles by letting it on the face dry.

19. Butterflies and ladybugs bring messages of gifts. They tell of presents to come into your life. Sit still for a moment, with your eyes closed tight. Then see an image of the gift to come, with your second sight.

20. Move with intent the clouds in the sky. Make a hole in them if you can. This is a good way to measure and with practice, increase the power your intent can release.

21. Laugh every day so resources can flow. Be silly and funny, as a child would play. If your window is open and your house is clean, we will come in to help you laugh – though our influence is unseen.

Awakening the Power of Gemstones

SIGILS TO BE SIGNED
WHEN CALLING ANGEL NAMES

Ruby

Sapphire

Diamond

Opal

Garnet

Amethsyt

Beryl

Citrine

Topaz

Emerald

Aquamarine

Aventurine

Angel Names for Gemstones

1. Ruby   *Bichvaa-Hespit*

2. Garnet   *Alsbaa-Nusbit*

3. Topaz   *Trechbar-Nusvi*

4. Sapphire   *Isanak-Helsvi*

5. Amethyst   *Kursanat-eselva*

6. Emerald   *Alkbar-hurutver*

7. Diamond   *Aresknot-elestar*

8. Beryl   *Tretklenar-usetaa*

9. Aquamarine   *Aruksa-blave*

10. Opal   *Pifibri-setalvi*

11. Citrine   *Mechpafur-nesvi*

12. Aventurine   *Kariknat-utrabit*

Incantation:
Esepa usut klanuva

Let the power within awaken

Part Two

The Magic of the Fairies from Lyra

Visits by Fairy Folk from Lyra

On October 26, 2006, thousands of beings of the fairy realms came to Earth from the ancient constellation of Lyra. In the early days of November, I was visited by some of these endearing and magical fairy folk. A few are described below (see Color Plates 1-4 for sketches).

Fairy Woman
The beautiful little being appeared stark naked, except for a beautiful headdress that sparkled, curving over her forehead. She turned her head and looked at me with wide-set green eyes. There was an invitation in her pretty face. Afterwards, I asked one of the goddesses what she wanted and why she was naked. The answer was: "She always prefers being naked and she wants you to come and visit."

Elf Woman with Baby
She stood silently before me, her baby in a carrier. She wanted me to take in every detail – perhaps she knew before I did, that I would want to make a sketch of her. She was rosy-cheeked; her hair dark blonde. The details of her clothing were in contrast to the nakedness of the fairy from before. The patchwork skirt had the seams facing

to the outside, making little ridges around each patch. She was what we would consider "chubby", with a little stubby nose.

Male Fairy, "Green"

I saw a handsome looking male fairy in a tight-fitting grey and green suit. The pants ended at the knees; little hose and soft shoes completing the outfit. He sang the song he had brought me and jumped up and down with excitement when I spoke to him.[7]

Gremlin

The gremlin at first showed only his head in profile. The full face from the front, he came to show me two days later. He had a specific purpose for visiting me: Gremlins had a very poor reputation (as did goblins). They were viewed with some suspicion by the Earth's fairy folk as they arrived in large numbers from Lyra. Would they be pranksters or would they instead bring blessings? The gremlin had come to tell me that they were the bringers of wisdom to the higher beings of the cosmos, including those among human kind of higher consciousness.

Goblin

Whereas the gremlin had long straight grey hair and a pointed chin, the goblin had spiked red hair and a square chin. Goblins apparently work in the dark; and he wore strange little sunglasses when he showed me his face. Goblins bring wisdom to lower evolutionary lines of creatures, such as animals. This also includes the portion of humanity that chooses to live as though illusion still existed – those in lower consciousness.

Fairy, "Pink"

One morning, while one of the masters and I were having breakfast, we were surprised to hear a small voice coming from the vicinity

---

7 See "The Fairy Song", page 23

of her plate. It was a fairy by the name of "Pink", sitting on a tiny chair inside a raspberry. She asked us to be careful not to break her chair; so we carefully placed the raspberry on a saucer and put it in a protected spot.

Troll

One afternoon while I was scanning for secrets, I found myself in a troll's home. I apologized for the interruption and left, but he followed me into the room where we were working. As his tongue was too large for his mouth, he was continually drooling or spitting. He was very polite, though, and quite apologetic when he accidentally spat on my water bottle.

The Fairy Song: "Arlu Praveesh Parhem"

On the night of the 8th of November, 2006, a little male fairy came to my house to give me a song called Arlu Praveesh ("ee" sound as in "eat") Parhem. I asked him the following questions:

Q. What is your name?

A. Green

Q. Can you tell me about the song?

A. Your words are hard, hard.

Q. Do you mean it's hard to communicate with me?

A. Yes, hard, hard, hard.

Q. Is the song in preparation for the Fairy Magic that is soon to come from the fairies from Lyra?

A. Yes, yes, yes. It is so exciting!

(Just then my phone rang and he asked if he could wait on my back porch. I said yes; I would call him after my conversation.)

Questions continued....

Q. What does this song do? Is it to unlock the flow of information?

A. It is a mystery, mystery, mystery.

Q. You mean I have to wait before understanding it till it's the right moment?

A. Yes. This is so exciting!

Q. I am excited too. Thank you. Am I doing it right? (The song was not in any scale I was familiar with)

A. Yes, yes, yes.

On November 13th, the thousands of fairies from Lyra who gathered here on earth, shared their magic spells with us. It was then that I realized the purpose of this little song: it removed the protective shield that surrounds the incantations, so that I would be able to hear them.

"ARLU PRAVEESH PARHEM"
(LYRICS)

Avra vru ash. Ash vrash oo nee-va aru hem.
Ista var vi, Ista var vi. Klaru Hem.
Bich tra nu ram para vish tra u ram
Bel-a vis vi vela. Sil bi his vra ura.
Bel esh nut vra ba. Bel es nut vri aruvish pra-va.
Arla pra veesh parhem
Run setvi par lu vi bra nish parhem.
Tra ur sa ba lu vish par hem
Vi lis tra ush na vis tri kla ru hem.
Spel a vi, Spel a vi, oo vas vri tre na bi.
Gel vi as vra ba ur
Stra u mish pa u stra kla na tur.

"ARLU PRAVEESH PARHEM"

Figure 2

The Pronunciation of the Fairy Language

For those who speak a Germanic language, the pronunciation is easier. It is as though you are reading German, with the exception of the "v". The syllables are pronounced with equal value: "Ba-ra-vek", for example, has equal emphasis on every syllable.

Pronunciation:
a – as in pardon
e – as in beckon
o – as in border
u – as in true
ch – as in the German, "buch" (or "kh")
ee - as in please
aa -as in spa
v-as in Victor
sh-as in ship
w- as in wide

They don't use percentages; the percentage is seen in the mind as a partial apple or other object like a pie. The fairy language has no past or future tense, since only the moment exists.

THE ALPHABET OF THE DWARFS FROM LYRA

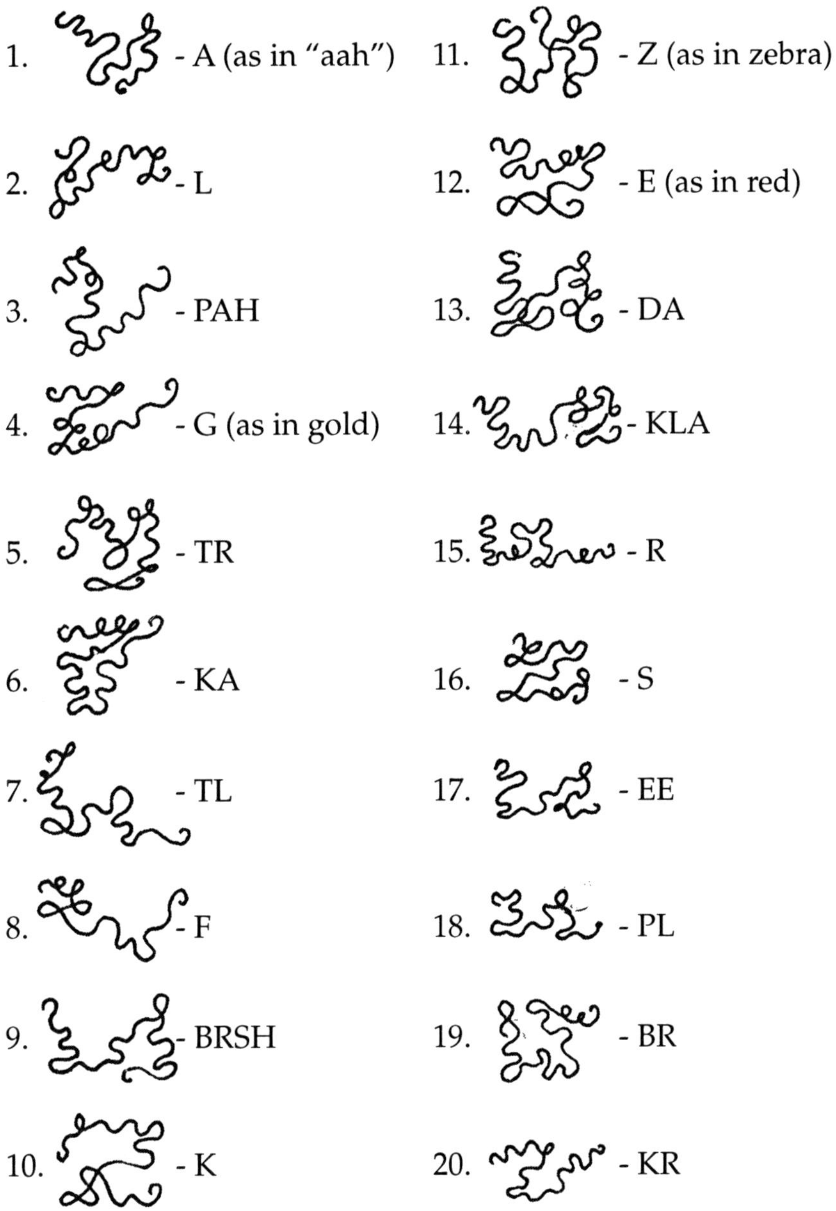

1. — A (as in "aah")

2. — L

3. — PAH

4. — G (as in gold)

5. — TR

6. — KA

7. — TL

8. — F

9. — BRSH

10. — K

11. — Z (as in zebra)

12. — E (as in red)

13. — DA

14. — KLA

15. — R

16. — S

17. — EE

18. — PL

19. — BR

20. — KR

Figure 3

THE ALPHABET OF THE DWARFS FROM LYRA

21.  ⟨symbol⟩ - SH

22.  ⟨symbol⟩ - V

23.  ⟨symbol⟩ - M

24.  ⟨symbol⟩ - N

25.  ⟨symbol⟩ - B

26.  ⟨symbol⟩ - VRA

27.  ⟨symbol⟩ - U (as in true)

28.  ⟨symbol⟩ - P

29. 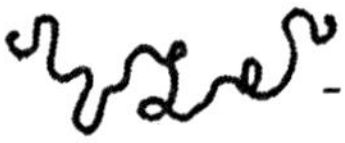 ⟨symbol⟩ - H

30.  ⟨symbol⟩ - ISH

31.  ⟨symbol⟩ - BE (as in bed)

32.  ⟨symbol⟩ - A (as in art)

33.  ⟨symbol⟩ - BL

34.  ⟨symbol⟩ - I

35.  ⟨symbol⟩ - D

36.  ⟨symbol⟩ - F

37. 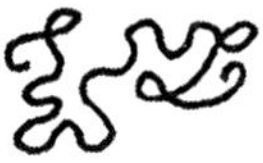 ⟨symbol⟩ - O (as in cross)

38.  ⟨symbol⟩ - BLU

39.  ⟨symbol⟩ - KRA

40.  ⟨symbol⟩ - T

Figure 3 (continued)

THE ALPHABET OF THE DWARFS FROM LYRA

41. ![symbol] - TRA

42. ![symbol] - BLE

43. ![symbol] - VR

44. ![symbol] - LA

45. ![symbol] - CH

46. ![symbol] - SP

47. ![symbol] - VI

48. ![symbol] - HE

49. ![symbol] - OO

50. ![symbol] - SA

51. ![symbol] - VA

52. ![symbol] - BRA

53. ![symbol] - UR

54. ![symbol] - NU

To put together three letters, as in "red":

Figure 3 (continued)

THE ALPHABET OF THE DWARFS FROM LYRA

Numerals

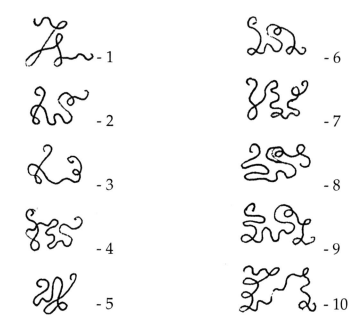

- 1
- 2
- 3
- 4
- 5
- 6
- 7
- 8
- 9
- 10

Figure 3 (continued)

Fairy Magic from Lyra

Tranuvech Pelenor u stratnava hereshvi. Ne-urishva paluna. Kre u vra hereshvi. Unut varuklem. Pre nut pre vas parvi. Stech va uvra het. Pel nus varum brish barvi. Klet vaar uset.

From far we have come. To tell you the codes. It is our gift to you. We wish to reside here. Our joining together our paths with yours will make all life flourish. Stretch your mind this day, include us in your sight.

Esh ma neesh vi ra vel, vru asbi stela hur. Kel afvra ba urutvi klesh ma nur varu bish manu resh. Estra mach mi ner va vu keles vaa. Pret sut balush vel ska u la vraa.

Give now your ear and we shall say the words to speak. They open the codes of the heart, that bring that which you desire into form. Through the magic of fairies build a new life:

Brush aa vala vrit
Pru a nes pelu kraa
Heres vir nus parvit
Belch avru saa

Mi sulvi baresvi
Kla nur pri u saa
Belshuvanar velchvi
Rut set viles vaar

Peresh vel u satvavi
Krich barut bresh braknaa

El huf pre u selvavi
Gru staboch perus vanaa

Kel u stri nen hurvelevi
Sta u michpre nun hersvaa
Gru va ur menunit
Heles virsh urs pravaa

Gu staa u bra efbi
Berush virsk prevaa
Garu neesh bel es efrubi
Gel stru ar nu vaach.

Paar u na presh pra vuch. Vru a buruski bel a nush. Sti arnervat kel vis bra usut. Gra stra u sabervi esh tra ulmirat.

Impart not these words to those of impure thought. Keep them close to your heart. For when impurities enter the fairy group-mind through these words, fairies could die.

Granush vel es vravi heruspa ha. Krenug usva velesvi kresh tra hur varsaa stenura velch shpi keratu. Glu staber nen hersh pra u vataa.

It takes our trust to place this gift in your hands. But if you have been led to these words, we know your heart is true. Use them with respect for life.

Krechna uresvi klebaa staba ulavet.

Our energies are now blended with yours.

14 Spells of the Fairies from Lyra

The following pages contain fourteen spells gifted to us by the Fairies from Lyra. Each spell is shown in handwritten Fairy writing, followed by the transliteration and then the English translation.

The speed at which spells manifest is determined by the complexity of what is being created; the higher the complexity, the longer it takes. This is because complex objects must first be formed as a blueprint in the undisturbed space of other realms, or else only a hollow shell would form. Results achieved through spells also depend upon the practitioner.

SPELL # 1
TO BRING FORTH FORM

Es vaa trua, skel vu brach
Nunhur sarveesh trerurach
Bel a vees tra ve urespimarnuch
Pra u pra usbavi gerstraa plavuch

Ancient the words I speak this way
To bring to form the words I say
Shape now the image I see in my mind
Bring forth the form of one of its kind.

Bersh vel es vi trua vu vi
Krenu spaau ratvi kelesh varnu
Bruach vaar uras ple hus vasarvir
Kre usnat pel uchvi verblas plasavur

That which I speak is that which shall be
By the power of the words that are given to me

SPELL # 2
FOR THE RETURN OF YOUTH

Gelstra nu bla vish ura vechspi par ha
Glustras va urechvi utre utra vaa
Vel strach nun her brush ura plefbi parhaa
Min eres vis tra ublech travaa.

Come fill my cup with living water
That youth may return, that it be restored
Turn now this water I hold in my hand
To that which brings youth to the body of man.

Bersh vel es vi trua vu vi
Krenu spaau ratvi kelesh varnu
Bruach vaar uras ple hus vasarvir
Kre usnat pel uchvi verblas plasavur

That which I speak is that which shall be
By the power of the words that are given to me

SPELL # 3
FOR IMMACULATE CONCEPTION

Varskla veesh prava manu vi sut
Kel efba uvastra minur bel va sut
Gle shtri minunechvi aruvech peravi
Vel estravaa klu bastru selvich sparari

Create your own kind by calling a child
See the little one clearly in mind
Speak these words and immaculately conceive
A babe in your womb and pregnant you'll be.

Bersh vel es vi trua vu vi
Krenu spaau ratvi kelesh varnu
Bruach vaar uras ple hus vasarvir
Kre usnat pel uchvi verblas plasavur

That which I speak is that which shall be
By the power of the words that are given to me

SPELL # 4
FOR BEAUTY

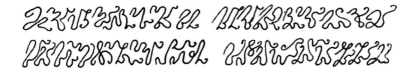

Kre na veesh ulechbi stauret
Velskrach ba uret vavi minuset
Kle sufba elesh preusbi pravaa
Belushvi tra usvrabaa granu speluvaa

A spell of beauty for all eyes to see
But you must believe and that you shall be
Others shall see your beauty renewed
Uplifted by the sight of the beauty of you

Bersh vel es vi trua vu vi
Krenu spaau ratvi kelesh varnu
Bruach vaar ures ple hus vasarvir
Kre usnat pel uchvi verblas plasavur

That which I speak is that which shall be
By the power of the words that are given to me

SPELL #5
FOR FLOWERS AND PLANTS

Ka na vush el stra blibratnavut
Vra ufba kre uch va spa rut nanuvut
Spla uvra eshvavi gel uva sperut
Nen tersh ulaefbi gerstra uvrasut

Flowers and plants will grow from these words
Bring beauty and joy as they flourish and grow
The flowers will last much longer than most
To life-force and magic they are hosts

Bersh vel es vi trua vu vi
Krenu spaau ratvi kelesh varnu
Bruach vaar ures ple hus vasarvir
Kre usnat pel uchvi verblas plasavur

That which I speak is that which shall be
By the power of the words that are given to me

SPELL # 6
FOR NEW SPECIES OF FLOWERS & PLANTS

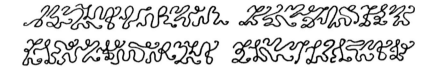

Tre u mish ble ur ratva ulech paravi
Skel achva tru eshvi ulech pres parvi
Gre ug minur kele vishbi starur
Klech bres ur bilatrech sur het klaravur

New species will form that have never yet been
Of flowers and plants never before seen
Speak these words to the seeds in your hand
When planted new flowers will cover the land

Bersh vel es vi trua vu vi
Krenu spaau ratvi kelesh varnu
Bruach vaar ures ple hus vasarvir
Kre usnat pel uchvi verblas plasavur

That which I speak is that which shall be
By the power of the words that are given to me

SPELL # 7
FOR ABUNDANCE

Bars hut pre su na neesh va tra
Ubelechspi pra u vra sta u nit perva
Klu bechspi minureesh tra u vaa
Sta ubelvich pelushvi stel avra vaa

Great abundance is yours
Like a river it flows
Speak these words and watch it grow
First it will trickle then it will pour
Speak them again whenever it slows

Bersh vel es vi trua vu vi
Krenu spaau ratvi kelesh varnu
Bruach vaar ures ple hus vasarvir
Kre usnat pel uchvi verblas plasavur

That which I speak is that which shall be
By the power of the words that are given to me

SPELL # 8
TO CALL IN A MATE

Selbi vavechspi uret vanabi
Gleg stuch ur na menu nit
Pars klut el esh varavi
Sta uch manunaa belesh va prit
Kle stug bel uresbi, kreug beresklaa
Traug varuspi ukrech manuraa

Call in the mate that you want in your life
Write down in detail what would make the mate right
Then over the fairy writing here given
Place the list of requirements written
Speak then the words with strength from the heart
The mate is then called, never to part

Bersh vel es vi trua vu vi
Krenu spaau ratvi kelesh varnu
Bruach vaar ures ple hus vasarvir
Kre usnat pel uchvi verblas plasavur

That which I speak is that which shall be
By the power of the words that are given to me

SPELL # 9
TO BRING ANSWERS

Kel vaa rutvi erch vaa uhursut
Mish tre bra as vaa urkret nan harsut
Bel ach vra uhursut kretnut hervavit
Kel esh stra uvanur brekrut nan hersut
Stra doch va uresbi nenhur varnavit

This spell awakens inspiration in you
It brings you answers, to know what to do
It brings light to a quandary, revealing the way
It helps you to know just what you should say
Still the mind when the words are spoken
That you may hear wisdom's instruction

Bersh vel es vi trua vu vi
Krenu spaau ratvi kelesh varnu
Bruach vaar ures ple hus vasarvir
Kre usnat pel uchvi verblas plasavur

That which I speak is that which shall be
By the power of the words that are given to me

SPELL # 10
FOR FREEDOM FROM ILLUSION

Bers anu vik pers klaa uravesbi
Gru ech vi stara ruch vi aresvi
Nin hirsh tu urachvi klauset maru net
Bil eshvi tra nech vit klaur varnaset

Free another from illusion's grip
Over a photo or name speak it
The words that are given will freedom bring
Shake loose the bonds to which he clings

Bersh vel es vi trua vu vi
Krenu spaau ratvi kelesh varnu
Bruach vaar ures ple hus vasarvir
Kre usnat pel uchvi verblas plasavur

That which I speak is that which shall be
By the power of the words that are given to me

SPELL # 11
FOR STRENGTH IN OPPOSITION

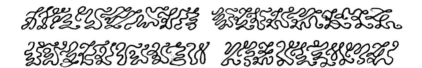

Ulesbi kra nu va vitch ula echbi starut
Bre sut va ures nu elechvi sta arut
Bi skaa ula es na tru ul vara vaa
Kel ech vi u ach vrabi starut spaa
Menes sta uritvi keleshvi u staraa

Stand firm in the face of another's opposition
These words will give strength whenever they're spoken
The strength to know when to stand or to yield
When spoken they give you power to wield

Bersh vel es vi trua vu vi
Krenu spaau ratvi kelesh varnu
Bruach vaar ures ple hus vasarvir
Kre usnat pel uchvi verblas plasavur

That which I speak is that which shall be
By the power of the words that are given to me

SPELL # 12
FOR HARMONY

Kle u vich vas urechpi staurat
Mish tra uvanesvi krechpa arurat
Skelu la u tra mish veres tra u va
Nin klu veres tra u va beles tru a mispa

To replace discord with harmony
Bring this magic to the strife
All shall dissolve instantly
That is not filled with light

Kras na sterutvi kla ushbaa heruvit
Stel uch vi u aresba helsut veruvit

But if it persists, cease to resist
For then it is meant to be
Then an insight is hidden waiting for you to see

Bersh vel es vi trua vu vi
Krenu spaau ratvi kelesh varnu
Bruach vaar ures ple hus vasarvir
Kre usnat pel uchvi verblas plasavur

That which I speak is that which shall be
By the power of the words that are given to me

SPELL # 13
TO RESTORE BALANCE

Tra u ma vash ulu echbi klabusat
Vira nutvi kleush baranut trausat
Trauch bla blu va vestri elusat
Bla hutva tre u nish parvusat
Tre achbi mi lu blava ustra varbat

Restore the balance to the one in your mind
Say his name three times and you will find
That balance of emotion and mind as well
Will return to the one whom you help with this spell

Bersh vel es vi trua vu vi
Krenu spaau ratvi kelesh varnu
Bruach vaar ures ple hus vasarvir
Kre usnat pel uchvi verblas plasavur

That which I speak is that which shall be
By the power of the words that are given to me

SPELL # 14
FOR A BENEFICIAL OUTCOME

Knuch auvastra kla unet varabich
Bresh bra ma vuhet ul klet vra mastrich
Vel usvra verhat ush vra uvestra perdu
Mi es bla unesh veesh pravutaa para nos stravu

To change a path that will lead to ill
A course of action that is not of divine will
Speak these words and you can re-arrange
To a beneficial outcome all will change

Bersh vel es vi trua vu vi
Krenu spaau ratvi kelesh varnu
Bruach vaar ures ple hus vasarvir
Kre usnat pel uchvi verblas plasavur

That which I speak is that which shall be
By the power of the words that are given to me

Photos of the Fairies

Figure 4

A close-up of a wood fairy with outstretched wings fills this photo. The body is the darker blue-grey vertical part just to the right of center; the head at the top has a bark crown (instead of hair. The round globes are small fairies (elementals).

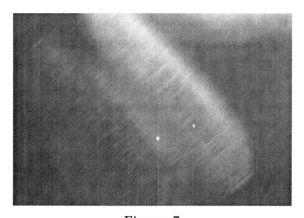

Figure 5

A close up of fairy wings

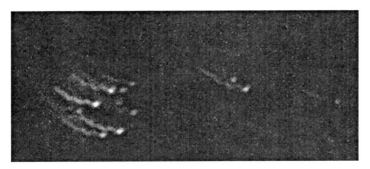

Figure 6

When we asked what the picture had captured, a fairy replied "Andromedan Fairies flying speedy".

For color photos go to www.spiritualjourneys.com and click on View Interdimensional Photos

Part Three

The Magic of the
Earth-Fairies from Lyra

Ancient Keys Restored

The Earth originated from the Antares star system. As part of Antares, the Earth played a most important role: it housed the cosmic life-force center. The Antares star-system was governed by two kings.

The life-force center of the cosmos had many unimaginable assets and was an inexhaustible energy source. The kings of Antares found that they could use it as a negotiable commodity; and in so doing, they became some of the wealthiest and most powerful kings in the cosmos.

Those that came to barter for its power, left with an amazing tool: The Power of Ytolan. With it, cities of great magnificence could be built in a single afternoon with thought.[8]

As the pillaging of the cosmic life-force center continued, the Earth (then the host planet to the life-force center) continued to fall in consciousness. One of the kings eventually moved the life-force center to the main planet where his palace was located. Those that existed in its proximity had constant rejuvenation and everlasting life.

The Earth, now deprived of her destiny and stripped of her light and power, became an outcast as she plummeted in consciousness. In the

8 For more information see "The Power of Ytolan" in *Secrets of the Hidden Realms*, page 142

ages of separatism, opposite light repelled. Stripped of her glory, the Earth was repelled out of the Antares system and eventually ended up, in her fallen state of consciousness, within our star-system.

When this occurred, it was decided within the fairy realms that 10% of the fairies would leave for Lyra, carrier of the cosmic "pineal gland" or the 7th chakra. They would stay connected with the Earth's fairies - the 90% that fell in consciousness, remaining on Earth to keep our planet from becoming devoid of nature's beauty.

Staying "connected" meant that they did not intermingle with the fairies of Lyra; and that they kept their language intact (see Figure 3, Earth Fairy Language). They used a different form of magic than the fairies of Lyra – old Earth magic. By keeping their identity as Earth fairies, they would provide a life-line to their fallen fellow fairies as follows:

1) They would stay connected to the same grid (previously an array of lines of light along which information flowed, telling species how to behave), feeding it with higher consciousness so that the Earth's fairies would not lose their magic abilities altogether.

2) They would have in safekeeping the higher secrets and keys of earth-magic, which would inevitably be lost on Earth during its plummet in consciousness. Then, when the Earth would one day assume her glory again[9], these keys would be restored as the fairy realms from Earth would one day reunite.

3) The seat of magic is in the pineal gland, the seventh chakra. The fact that the 10 percent would reside in the location of the cosmic seventh chakra, would maximize their magic as well as the contribution they provided to their counterparts on Earth.

9 Described in *The Ring of Truth*

EARTH FAIRY LANGUAGE

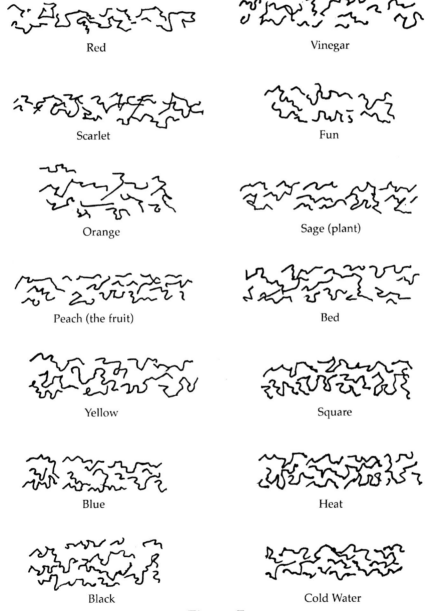

Red	Vinegar
Scarlet	Fun
Orange	Sage (plant)
Peach (the fruit)	Bed
Yellow	Square
Blue	Heat
Black	Cold Water

Figure 7

The Closing of the Circle

The fairies that came here from Lyra on the 26th October 2006, were not part of the 10 percent; they were quite simply fairies from Lyra. Including hundreds of thousands of elves and gremlins, dwarfs and goblins, they numbered two million four hundred thousand.

To understand why they came, preceding even the "earth–fairies" from Lyra, we need to know that the Earth has assumed a pivotal role within the cosmos[10]. The Goddess of all Creation has taken up residence on Earth.

Previously, separation consciousness was studied and the chakras were separated into different locations. But now we have entered into a state of cosmic inclusiveness and unity within diversity. It is therefore time to unite all chakras into a unified chakra field[11].

Because the embodiment of Mother is taking place on Earth, this is the location for their re-unification. The first to come on October 6, 2006 was the life-force center from Antares. It combined with the much smaller life-force center of the Earth[12], now located above Mother's throne. The throne is in Mother's palace, currently visible only to the eyes of some.

Next, the seventh chakra of the cosmos arrived, along with multitudes of fairies and other little beings, from Lyra.

On the 13th November 2006, a long-awaited event occurred: From the star system of Lyra, 50,000 fairies arrived on Earth; all originally from Earth before the fall. With their advent, a great gift was given.

As the cosmos entered a golden and indefinite period of light in August 2006, 10 percent of humanity still clung to the appearance of illusion. The role of fairies and elves had always been to hold the obsolete until it could be transmuted to light. When 10 percent of

10 Described in *Secrets of the Hidden Realms* and *The Ring of Truth.*
11 See *Journey to the Heart of God.*
12 Previously located in a temple in the crust of the earth

our fairies and elves left for Lyra, they took 10 percent of unresolved portions of light on Earth with them. With their arrival, a massive clearing of the denser portions on Earth took place.

The fairy, Planechbirskbrakpravprekhuruset was called to oversee this large scale clearing. When I spoke to the new arrivals, they said, "We are too busy to talk today. Can we talk secrets during your pretend[13] tomorrow morning? Today is a new dance for a new today."

The Queen of the Fairy Queens

With the new beginnings in the cosmos, a new fairy Queen of Queens had to be instated. Her taking form and the role she played in the re-uniting of the Earth's fairies began in September 2006.

It was in the third week of September that the palace of the Mother first became visible to those who can perceive energy directly. During that week I was instructed to conceive babies immaculately. Immaculate conceptions weren't new to me; several of the female masters in my classes had been assisted into pregnancy with immaculate conceptions. The first little boy was already several months old and some that were pregnant were women in their sixties. The gestation period was always ten or ten and a half months long.

After the conception, I did not have much time to consider it further, as both my teaching schedule and cosmic assignments increased. When in Indiana during the second week of October 2006, I began experiencing physical symptoms that resembled the early stages of labor. To my query as to what was going on, I was told that it was time to deliver, that ten months had passed since the conception in September.

---

13 Time is just an obsolete illusion at this point.

Time has ceased to exist, but even the illusion of there being time is very different on Earth than anywhere else. We are like the child in the middle of the merry-go-round who, sitting over the pivot point, feels that the merry-go-round is going very slowly. But for the children on the outer edge, it is going at a dizzying speed. For us, only a few weeks had passed, but it had been the equivalent of ten months.

The number of fetuses conceived by me had been eight. Four were transferred (as previously agreed) to the lead Indigo child on Earth, Melissa (25 years old). I went into labor and Melissa's water broke, while still in class. Soon after closing class, we were driven to Ohio, where at 1:00 a.m. the next morning, first my delivery and then hers took place in a hotel room. I had never experienced a natural child-birth, whereas Melissa had previously delivered three children with a mid-wife's assistance, and she was able to help us both through the experience.

During the following weeks, the babies were transported back and forth between me in Oregon and Melissa in Toronto. I breastfed for most of the hours of the night; and she watched them during the days. However, she could see and touch them and I could not.[14]

Wrapped in blankets, they held their shape, so that I knew where the little mouth was to suckle. I could feel them suckle and noticed that the one in the teddy bear blanket always bit on my nipple when she fell asleep.

I cried over the babies I could not see. According to Melissa, they grew rapidly. Soon they did not need breastfeeding anymore. Each night after falling asleep with the bottle, Thoth and the Goddess Sarah would transport them to the eight cribs I had set up in one of my bedrooms - they needed to be near me for at least half the day.

---

14 The babies were inter-dimensional god-babies who were primarily in the etheric but at times also interacted in the physical. Melissa can see etheric bodies.

We wanted very much to capture them on film. Fifteen rolls of film later and several Polaroid attempts, we managed to film two of them on a video camera.[15]

The 13th November 2006 marked the arrival of the "Earth-Fairies" from Lyra. I was in a hotel sitting room in Toronto with 10 female masters (3 pregnant with immaculate babies), and Melissa with the 8 little ones. We had difficulty keeping them in their cribs, as they tended to levitate when asleep. Suddenly the little girl (we called her "Little Heart" because her blanket had little pink hearts on it) levitated and exited the room through a mirror.

I immediately spoke the incantations of Mother's white magic[16] to bring her back. I continued for what seemed like quite a long time; but she still wasn't coming back. Instead, the rooms filled with masses of fairies returning to Earth. The light turned gold; the feeling was so intense that some of the women wanted to pass out, or felt icy cold or boiling hot.

Only after the fairies poured in, did Little Heart return. We were informed at that time that she was the Queen of Fairy Queens, and had gone to summon the fairies.

Little Heart, and other inter-dimensional god-babies being birthed at this time, are weaving two realities together like a needle stitching a tear. They are merging our world with a world in which Mother's majestic palace stands, where fairies can be seen and god-babies can be cuddled.

---

15 Unfortunately, I was not able to obtain permission to publish the photos in this book.
16 See the "Ring of White Magic" in *The Ring of Truth*

A Message from the Earth-Fairies from Lyra

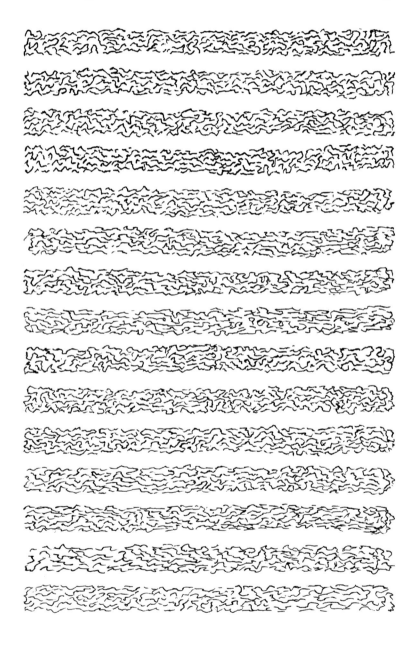

Hirsk sklabu varet birskva urs nanuvet. Belsh tri askva ureskla urnut biles bruk. Pilsh natva uresbi skla uvra vranavilsk. Bri stra uvra viles va ruk trekva varinisk.

Birchva uru heshpi klinknit helshpa uruvi vrskrekpa ruvla vikspi uruch vi aranesk. Kelstru kelba eruvechspi klaunakva vilesvi trechba urechshpa vravranuk vertlpa. Kel echspri minuveshpi tra subaluk nikpre.

Gelspriakva truechspi habalesk uvra aa. Nelgurk gre truachvi. Pelshprk nanuhart garuvechvi staurak parpratl ve uvrava. Hershtra nunhurs travalisbi erchna sutlva ursva.

Gershstra urech vanablik, berstla uluch herstrava bavaplik. Nush tra urechbi pravaspu hersblabak unechbi sparluk.
Satlhuf arabi kletsut manarek bel achvrabakspelvi. Striknat su bechspi, virinak ertlvi. Presparut elshminuk va kletsut kravunak.

Velstra ubla velchspi sparek nun hersh vravi starek nunhertlvrnavak stare bilsk vriskraa.

Translation
That which was taken must be returned.
From ages gone by the keys be restored.
Bring forth the message: The ring must close.
Rally the lost ones and bring them home.

From each a gem unsurpassed,
Will glow in the crown of the Goddess Supreme.

And when they are joined the activation begins
Of the power of magic that fairies once held.
The story repeated through eons of time;
That all may remember the powers sublime;
That all may heed the call when it comes
From stars far and near as has long been planned
Through the portal of Virnsk and the child holds the key.

Establish first one, then the others will come.
First 21 keys, then 34 more. Then follow 55
And then 89. 102 and 203 must follow after.

Guard well these words, for a mystery is told
Of the secrets of magic only fairies can hold.

30 Names and Meanings of the Earth-Fairies From Lyra

All beings in the cosmos that have distinguished themselves in their roles or assigned tasks are given a meaning after their name. This is a badge of honor and respect, a mark of distinction. It is always also a description of either their roles or, as in this case, their natures.

1. **Enturalisecondanimiragenilokannavennahyeh**: She who brings glad tidings
2. **Erlinochbreshenbrocherinbokbreklespoch**: She who brings the aura of mystique
3. **Sperlidochenblishenochberlienklblikendoch**: She who dazzles with magical beauty
4. **Klishpakeldabelendochalbialdielenba**: She who sings the children to sleep

5. **Arleberenbershpasutberlipasutsaba**: She who shimmers like a thousand suns

6. **Breckldochsprekldornenklbreckenenkldorn**: She who has the colors of butterfly wings

7. **Shekarpakemoshemkaremsplakaroshemnokremsha**: She who trails stars in her wake

8. **Perinspaberlisutbershpaberinkerlisut**: He who watches from high thermals

9. **Belendisherskadorfbalendochershenoch**: She who spins the dreams

10. **Hershendorfblenebershenenklehemblenedochellendorf**: She who sparkles like a thousand suns

11. **Berenechberendornenkldorferindorn**: She whose voice delights all ears

12. **Arklibarliberenblishperliberlibarliklish**: She who gathers the morning prayers

13. **Furliburliberenesherliberliburlibesh**: She who trails rainbows

14. **Vrochnosztawiearamabearachtaneichtonokarareiszenkaru-makbarpaluchnaramaruyanaazpachalawanzana**: He who brings laughter to tired eyes

15. **Kerlidabershemdaberenbersklierlida**: He whose mirth enlivens all

16. **Duhklakdeenavondastarundatekneedarbalukdovabreskit-vindytek**: She who bathes nature in green light

17. **Urlinberskierinbraberlenerskielinda**: He who carries the golden ray of strength

18. **Sperlidochenblishenochberlienklblikendoch**: The one who dreams in new flowers

19. **Grimvahutrikipraperiblishnentipraktamianaksatviklak-takinablishminhabrah**: The bringer of abundant beauty

20. **Vechlaukeplasechokemchavechochtechlakemnoshenka**: The one who gathers life force to disperse to nature
21. **Sperklindaberindoherindobaherinkla**: The one who gathers life force to disperse to animals
22. **Erlikurliberlieshklespabespaerlibesh**: The one who carries messages among the stars
23. **Prinechspravatshikelatururumasprach**: The one who delights the eye with magic
24. **Sikarivatumkestoumkeratelumvanurkel**: The one who sings the song of mystery
25. **Runumriristriklinatuemplset**: The one who whispers the oceans' secrets
26. **Shtaakenoffragentaroffgalentakaptakinholograndishtish-magalinkaroe**: The one who keeps the story of the ring
27. **Perinspaberlisutbershpaberinkerlisut**: The one who consoles babies with love
28. **Bershiberliberendaerliberliberenda**: The one with pristine purity
29. **Kainasatvilochtrunaminechprikosala**: The one who dances through life, creating flow on the way
30. **Kriterastikelamminochprasetkivetchirkulam**: The one whose laughter awakens forgotten dreams

A Conversation with an Earth-Elf from Lyra

He approached the Indigo Child, Melissa, when we were together in a class in Toronto. He had tried to get my attention unsuccessfully and said:

"Excuse me. I need to write a letter. Can you help? It's a very important piece. The white lady isn't listening and my writing is small...

This is the letter here when I am talking, but my friends are not here and nobody can talk to me... because they give me funny faces and fly away.

I cannot fly like them – my arms are made of wood. Can I please have some friends back? If you can send for them all, that is OK. But if you please, *(at least)* one or two: Their names are P. Green and J. Green.

My name, if you please, is H. Brown.

Thank you, thank you sincerely."

I then asked what type of beings they were, and what type he was. He insisted that his reply be written:

"Dear Ma'am,

It is more formal to write letters because I am of respect. Those ones who make the faces and fly, are called funny looking elves with wings. I am of course, an elf who is modest. There are no feathers on my back.

Could you find those friends? I only have four dax (presumably elf money*), and you have dollars and cents. I am a poor man in your rich world.*

I will sign off now, because there is no more in my mind to say."

65

I used the Mother's gift of White Magic to transport 2 elves of his own sort to his location.

"Holy moly! This is a wonderful day! Would you like a beetle sandwich for a return? I only eat the beetles that are dead of course. I made one with mustard. I am too happy to be hungry. Thank you, thank you thank you. Are you a hungry white lady for my sandwich? The end."

I responded that I send him my love and that his love in return is enough. He replied that he would love me as a friend; because "unfortunately" he was in love with a dwarf. He said that every time he tried to 'knock at his pretty lady's door', he was confronted by a very "rude" male dwarf who was standing in his way. He concluded by saying, "Perhaps I shall bring crackers for him next time. Sometimes distraction is very useful.

One day I will be back; but today I should put on a pot of soup for friends. I am a good cook, you know. That is all. Thank you. Goodbye."

21 Earth-Fairies from Lyra are Assigned Hobbies

After arriving on the 13th November, one of the fairies informed me that she and 20 other fairies had sparkly shoes. She went on to say that, as soon as Mother assigned them hobbies, their shoes would have various colors.

On the 14th November, Mother assigned hobbies to the twenty-one fairies as follows:

During that specific week, five new fairy languages would come to Earth with the groups of fairies from different star-systems. Five of the fairies were to learn these languages and teach them to the other Earth Fairies, including the Earth-Fairies from Lyra that spoke the same language as the fairies on Earth.

Another five of the fairies were to gather the histories of the five newly-arrived groups. The histories were to be compiled, and kept in one location.

Five fairies were called to be matchmakers between fairies from the various different groups, ensuring that the protocols from both groups were considered in courting and marriages. Both parties also had to be made aware of what was expected of them as the spouse of a fairy from another group.

Five fairies were to plan regular parties for all groups of fairies to attend. This would promote camaraderie, romance and friendly relations. Again, social protocols had to be studied and incorporated into the festivities.

One fairy was assigned as the "new" historian and keeper of records and documents. A whole new era of interaction between the fairy groups was beginning, signifying unity within diversity. It is important that a common history, as well as a repository of contracts, be established regarding the interaction of these groups.

Thoth, The Crown and the Fairies

After the joyous return of the Earth-Fairies from Lyra, the suite in Toronto where I was working filled with fairies. They were also outside the windows. A strange golden glow hung around the hotel suite; we could hardly breathe. Some of the female masters with me lay on the floor overwhelmed with dizziness.

Thoth suddenly appeared outside our tenth-floor window. He was holding the partial crown of Mother in his hand; and we realized that each of the fairy groups was bringing a gem to construct her crown. We rushed to the window with cameras – but so did the fairies who also wanted to see.

Although we were able to catch a reasonably clear image of the two gems of her partial crown in his hand, we kept filming hundreds of little balls of light at the same time. At first the screen was just filled with white light on the digital camera, from their light. But then we held the lens of a pair of sunglasses over the camera lens and could capture the masses of fairies.

Thoth's large grey T-shirt (long enough to be like a tunic) showed up with enough detail to show the folds and distinguish the sleeves (see Color Plates 5-8, "Thoth, the Crown and the Fairies").

About the Photos in this Book:
It should be noted that none of the photos in this book has been "re-touched" in any way; and that the photographs came from at least three different cameras. We also experienced an interesting phenomenon: We were planning to use the digital files from the cameras for printing the photos in this book; but the files started to disappear within days. However, we were told that the images on the physical photos would not disappear; and so the photos in this book had to be scanned from prints we had previously made up for viewing purposes.

14 Spells of the Earth-Fairies from Lyra

SPELL #1
THE KEY TO START A SPELL

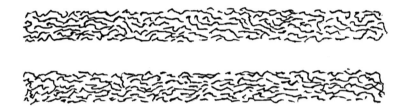

Bels brukvak blik breversbt hevelshvi akbar urklatvik
nerchst helshba urutvi heresba erskruklabi.
Vilnesk uret ble ufraba arha nurklitheres vilshtr ufba
ursklava rech varshbi uvalefbi vanurinsk.
Er klut birkspa huretpi klavavech spa-urara.

Forget not the ancient ways of yore
That which once was has been restored
By saying these words you open a door
The magic will flow for you to explore.

Say them before each spell that you do
And the magic of fairies will flow through you.

SPELL # 2
TO SATISFY HUNGER

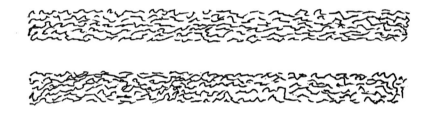

Kernakva hurik spa uvratbli asbaluk hesh tranik bliklatruk
virnahikprsva ursta blshna virskva utsabaluk.
Pelusvi utrabla usvanek.
Krus ablut sparva nuntreshva urkirksblavi sparut shpelsvaa.
Achvrasnut ulekra hirstadom branavit.

Come from the table and hunger no more
For that which you eat shall satisfy still
Feel the satiety and so it shall stay
For three meals long; what you call a day.

SPELL # 3
TO REVEAL YOUR CHARM

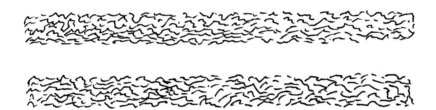

Gerchstrava barshnus helesvri vra skubaluk.
Perch nit vilisk britvelsh stravuba elekstriknavirsk vla usta
helsh pret prafblsk prishpra uvekspalbi klitra nus pretlufra
ba helshvi varshnit elekvi avestra blatnufaferbi.

From fairies' mouths this spell does come
To bring your charm to be seen by everyone.
Let joy be felt to be by your side
The charm you have will no longer hide.

Parek vilshvavi urabekspi valaluk
Min hur parvelshvi kranuk barnasut.

This spell must repeat; these words you say
As you awaken upon each day.

SPELL # 4
TO BRING FRIENDS

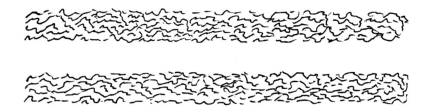

Nushbra urekbi alskva urek pri pratrnut kelsbaha nutvi.
Velskla uvra sut ba ru ek mina vra u velsh pra uversklava hur
la vik eles briknut pa u vlahu sparakletvirsh eleknu spelavra.

Speak these words to bring you friends
Those you can cherish; on whom to depend
Of like heart-energy call them to come unto you
A blessing they'll be, and you'll bless them too.

SPELL # 5
TO AVOID CALAMITY

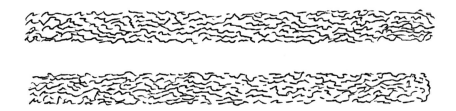

Varsvk urkslaminuvek spavaruk krasta blasut
Tre mish plauvravis pretpra hustra elekstra urhunut
Mesh tri uru ekbar uvrespa vilklarabrut prekspava
Kru niursta vilshprit heleskubris brat pravanus.

Carry this spell wherever you go
To avoid calamity that threatens to show
No longer at the mercy of the flow of another
Stay also, calamity, from the life of your brother.

SPELL # 6
TO OPEN THE PORTAL TO THE FAIRY WORLD

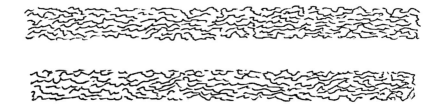

Paluk brak bristrava hushpelu akvra usba helevit.
Verskra uchblereshvi krasbru ekvarastru.
Kel avri elekstraha pluprek pra ureshbi skater marnavit
sklera ubuekla vilstra u briaknabelsksut.

Come follow the trail of these words with me.
They lead to our world so you may see
Through a portal the way of the fairy world.
Practice that you may remember the sight,
For your mind may deny what is yours by right.

SPELL # 7
TO LIGHTEN YOUR LOAD

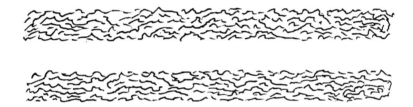

Varechsvl hasva urablikspa urek. Pertlahufstra
marnanekspi erla urtrabilesnik sklaraa.
Perkhurk velsklavaa usetvi pirklahus pelshplik
pretufla hures trahup peresnutvi veleskla.

Upon your back a heavy load;
but lighter now these words are told.
Lighter yet if you repeat it twice.
Lighter you'll be if you say them thrice.

SPELL # 8
TO GROW SEEDS

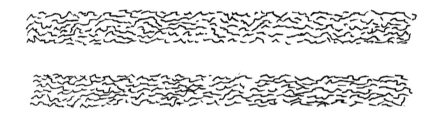

Gelva uvekstrahik manavek ekelsva retvi.
Briasva klusbra nun heresvik kra nu estra ulef
palesvu sklava ruretba huruk spatlvi.
Nechtri ash vares vla ursk kla huruvas par vi baranusk pletvatlha.

Grow your seeds and they shall be
Anything you want for them to be.
The same seeds can grow many plants you will find.
See them and hold them firm in your mind.

SPELL #9
TO PROTECT A CHILD

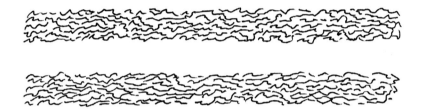

Birsna uretbi kilvig-nun harvasta.
Eksalbi uvlekspi kersul biles tra u varanit.
Kel achvra huresbi klashba truagnat varutreg.
Silbi nusva urva kluvabesh vi sarutrug nenvraa.

Shield your child's privacy.
Repeated once, these words prevent
The cruelty of others from piercing the shield.
Unnoticed by some is the child when in need;
Through the love of a parent form now the field.

SPELL #10
TO DISCERN THE TRUTH OF ANOTHER

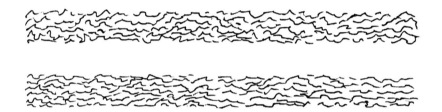

Haaknik peles kra u tur.
Virsknik velesh pravasur.
Graachnak elsva urs eres varvi.
Pelsh plek pra utnut spelech urs vrasvrus
pershpa pelech stra uvelesh hus nanuvrs.
Kra sut belch hirstra menenurs kelstra.

Follow another's path through his view
That you may discern his truth for you.
To understand his words to you
You must see his world through his own view.

SPELL #11
TO FIND WHAT YOU LOST

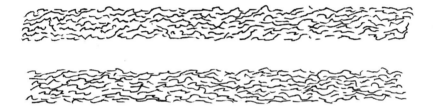

Varsk varnit veles vra uvraba, erk uklat
birskna hulhitsh virs kelespa.
Mir navael skla hufret ut ba urs.
Tre ukva el satru bilsh natvat berestru.
Kla u ve piles hartva ernahit.

Find what you lost. Call it to you.
By these words it shall find its way back to you.
Call while you see the image you seek.
Your voice shall call it by the words you speak.

SPELL # 12
TO STRENGTHEN A SPELL

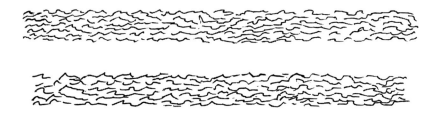

Gerch stranu valvelchspi uvra belsh abutra.
Pirs prak uvlavelchspi, usetvi kelesba ninhurs belechspa.
Nush blas bra us klenavit skel achva hers struraa.
Vrasklik belbra ushvraspurat helsut elech sutvesbi klavaa.

Speak these words over potions you make.
They only add good; they never can take.
Speak them therefore with good intent
In your own tongue, voice what you want at the end.

To speak it in verse, the outcome you state,
Will strengthen the spell in the potions you make.
Make them from flowers and oils very pure
This works well with spells from the fairy world.

SPELL #13
FOR LOSS

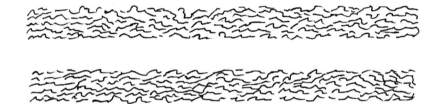

Kel es vra bi blak pra nunsu bribraket.
Pels nuchtri uvivra vi. Ska u valva dak.
Bersh nus hel sklararok spiartl hukvelsvrakra
Brik brat nut eles vivaklat uresvi harastu.
Pertl achvra varvahesh.

Find now in loss something of worth.
From something that's shed, let new now come forth.
Something is given for that which is taken
For that which has died, let something awaken.

SPELL #14
TO BRING STRENGTH TO ENDEAVORS

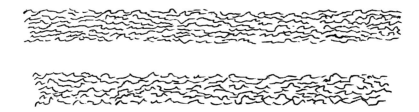

Gelstra urut hekkla ursvik blechbek selusetri
hersh trabaklut nusbi erkla utvirt stelbaa.
Stelalof virtl ursk manahech. Spil hersk
vir kla usvra ba uch vet ersh urtlavaa.

Bring strength to endeavors by enlisting our aid
Fairy folk come where these words are said.
They know that the one who speaks them thus,
Is either a friend or one of us.

Kres nukva belish presm hurs ut travaa.
Kel virs ur ustakldos erech varavi.

A friend to all life he must surely be
To have these words only fairies may see.

Part Four

The Magic of the Fairies
from Venus

The Arrival of the Fairies from Venus

In the early morning hours of 15th November, 62,000 fairies from Venus came to Earth to join the other fairy groups that were gathering in a verdant valley in the crust of the Earth (see Appendix I, "100 Fairies from Venus").

Their return to Earth was the catalyst for the cosmic heart center, which had been situated in Venus, to follow to earth as well. The heart of the cosmos was shut down by the beings that had once resided there. This was done when they ascended en masse as a civilization through the sun.[17]

17 See the "Realms of Arulu", page 148 in *Secrets of the Hidden Realms*

Fairy Potions From Venus

The following potions were gifted to us by the Fairies from Venus through Fairy Gosafasvtaaklrmaavarhxaui. She is the fairy in charge of teaching all other fairies how to teach humans through pleasant games and delightful tricks; in other words, how to trick humans into learning.

Information I was given about the potions:

1. The fairies said that these potions are *not* for consumption by humans.
2. They do not use measurements; and would not give us quantities. They said: "Use the ingredients according to taste." I asked, therefore, what they meant by "taste" – does that mean what feels right? The answer was, "Well, fairies do like to lick their fingers."
3. When I asked about the meaning of the different colors of magic as well as some of the ingredients, I was told I had to solve 15 mysteries for each recipe's secrets to reveal themselves. They were unyielding regarding this. The mysteries having been solved, there is an explanation following the recipe for each potion. The wording of these explanations came directly from the Fairies.
4. I asked whether all ingredients were available on Earth. She replied: "Only if you have eggs and sugar – do you have those?" (indicating that they are common household ingredients).

POTION 1: POTION FOR GREEN MAGIC

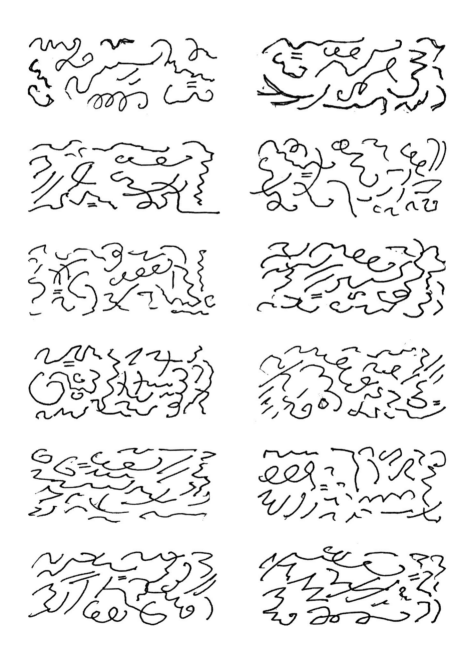

POTION FOR GREEN MAGIC

Mix and boil together:

Olive oil
Dandelion seeds
Lavender flowers
Thistle mush
Grass powder

Explanation of the Potion's Uses, Ingredients and Preparation

Green Magic is for all things natural, especially if it is broken.

If something is broken, i.e. a tree that falls after a storm, then you will want to make a big batch. If you want only to make a flower grow, you only need a small amount.

Because people are not fairies, they cannot eat this. If you will mix it and put it in a dish in your garden, we will eat it for you.

Thistle Mush is ground thistles. You will need 2 or 3, mixed with oil. You can use your olive oil because it is in your kitchen.

Grass Powder is dried grass ground into a fine powder.

You can store this potion at room temperature for 5-10 days.

POTION 2: POTION FOR RED MAGIC

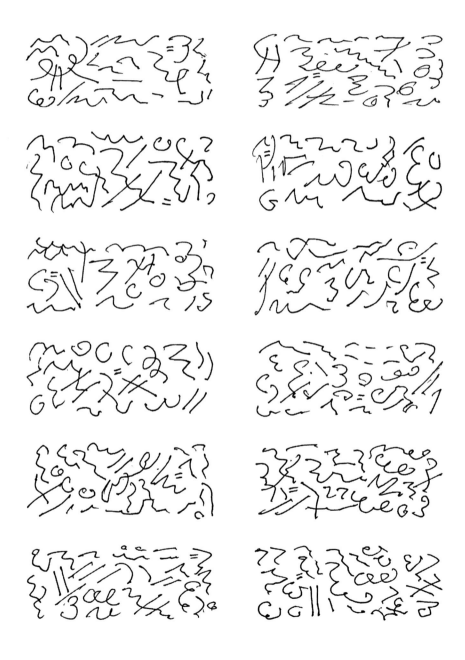

POTION FOR RED MAGIC

Mix and boil together:

> Bendover oil
> Dandelion leaves
> Dragon's blood
> Cherry juice
> Egg whites

Explanation of the Potion's Uses, Ingredients and Preparation

Red Magic is for if you are hurt or your friend is hurt; but it is not good to use for bones.

If you have a hurt leg, i.e., a cut or torn muscle, then you will want a big batch.

You can put this on your skin for up to 5 minutes of yours, and then please wash it off. It is not a good idea to put it on your cuts so only place it near the area.

I was relieved to hear that dragon's blood refers to the dragon's blood stone (presumably ground to a powder), a "sticky" stone that resembles a dried-up blood clot.

Bendover oil is lemon juice, oregano, chili powder, jasmine oil and parsley mixed with olive oil.

You can store this potion in your ice box or in the snow for 2 days.

POTION 3: POTION FOR BLUE MAGIC

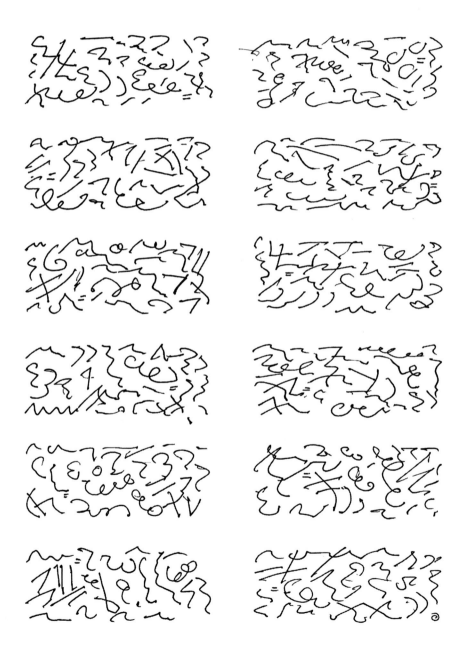

POTION FOR BLUE MAGIC

Mix together and boil:

Fish oil
Sea salt
Dandelion roots
Ocean water
Peppermint oil

Explanation of the Potion's Uses, Ingredients and Preparation

Blue Magic is for water. If your water is dirty or you need more water, you can make this, but make a lot please because it is delicious.

Because people are not fairies, they will feel sick to eat this. If you mix it up, you can put it in your bathtub or near a puddle and we will eat it for you.

This can be stored at room temperature for 15 days.

POTION 4: POTION FOR YELLOW MAGIC

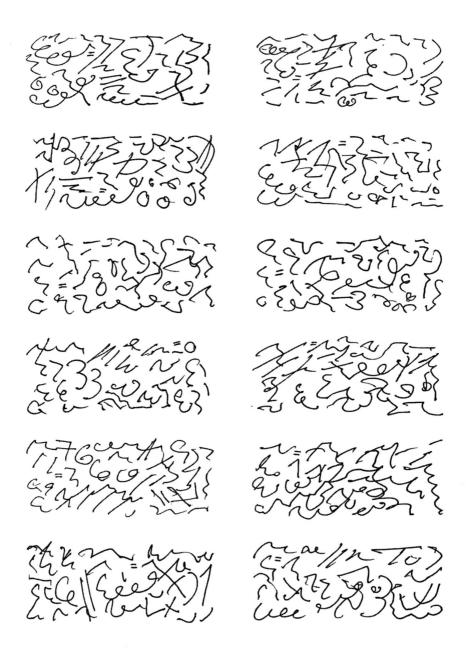

POTION FOR YELLOW MAGIC

Mix together and boil:

Olive oil
Dandelion flowers[18]
Cornstarch
Egg yolk
Sugar

Explanation of the Potion's Uses, Ingredients and Preparation

Yellow Magic is for remembering what you have forgotten or lost.

You can make a lot of this and sprinkle some in your hat and in your boots so you can remember.

You can store this in your ice box for 5-10 days.

---

18 I had painstakingly spent a day doing their intricate writing in each recipe. Suddenly the fairy working with me, said: "No, no, no! You made a very big mistake – you don't understand these potions at all!" When I asked what the problem was, she said I had left out the dandelion portions of each recipe. I had to go back through the writing and make the changes, indicating which dandelion parts to use.

POTION 5: POTION FOR ORANGE MAGIC

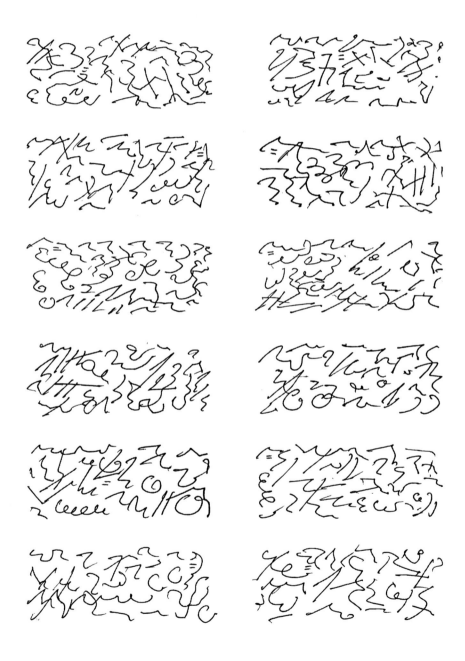

POTION FOR ORANGE MAGIC

Mix together and boil:

Olive oil
Rose water
Orange peel
Mugwort
Dandelion stem

Explanation of the Potion's Uses, Ingredients and Preparation

Orange Magic is for bones - if you have a broken one or if you need them strong. You can make a lot or a little, depending on the size of your bone.

You can place it on your skin, after you have mixed it, for up to 5 minutes and then please wash it off.

This can be stored at room temperature for 15 days.

POTION 6: POTION FOR PINK MAGIC

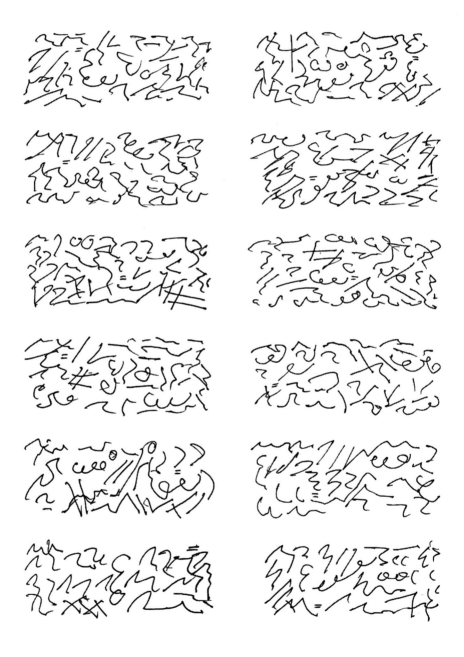

POTION FOR PINK MAGIC

Mix and boil together:

Olive oil
Peach juice
Sugar
Rose petals
Rose water
Dandelion flower
Dandelion root

Explanation of the Potion's Uses, Ingredients and Preparation

This is in case you have a lover, or you love your friends or you love yourself; because it is not a good idea to not express love. Please make a lot of this one because it is a very delicious dessert.

When you are mixing this, please remember to think of the ones you are loving and then please put it in a very beautiful bowl. You can set it out anywhere you like for 20 days; but please be aware that it probably won't last for 20 days, because we will eat it by then.

POTION 7: POTION FOR PURPLE MAGIC

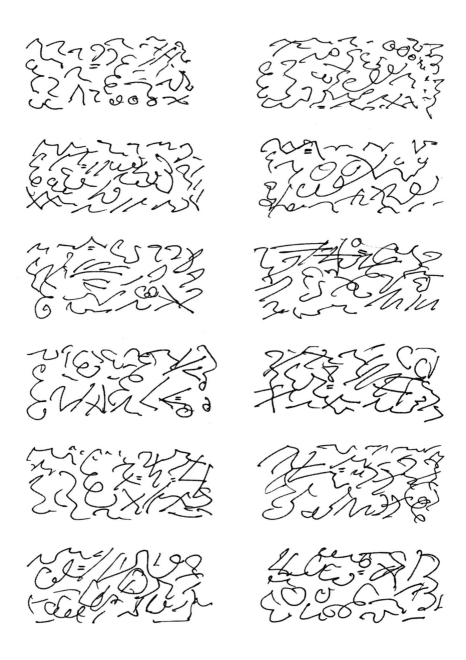

POTION FOR PURPLE MAGIC

Mix and boil together:

Olive oil
Bendover oil
Apple peel
Dandelion juice
Aloe vera

Explanation of the Potion's Uses, Ingredients and Preparation

Purple Magic is for when you have stress, or you are tired and you need to rest. It is good to mix this beside the Dream Magic potion if you are planning on going to bed.

After you have mixed it, place in a bowl and put beside your chair or beside your bed.

This should not be kept for longer than a day.

POTION 8: POTION FOR QUICK MAGIC

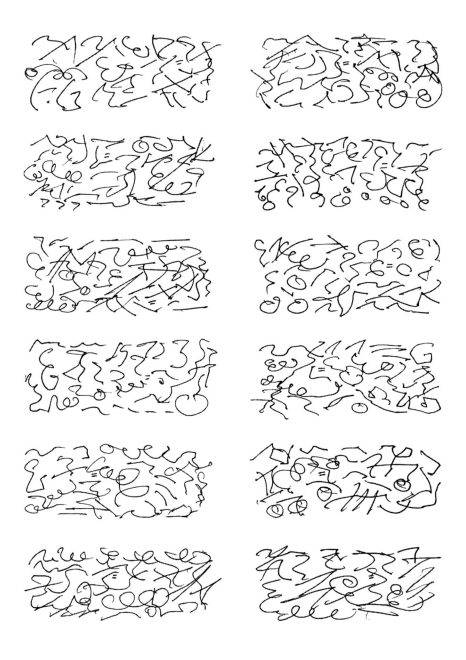

POTION FOR QUICK MAGIC

Mix only:

Olive oil
Lavender oil
House dust
Peanut butter
Honey

Explanation of the Potion's Uses, Ingredients and Preparation

Quick Magic is for when you need something done "speedy quick".

Mix these ingredients up very fast with your hand or a spoon. While you are mixing, think of what you want done. Place it on a bowl or a dish and we will eat it right away.

This should not be kept for longer than a day.

POTION 9: POTION FOR PLUG MAGIC

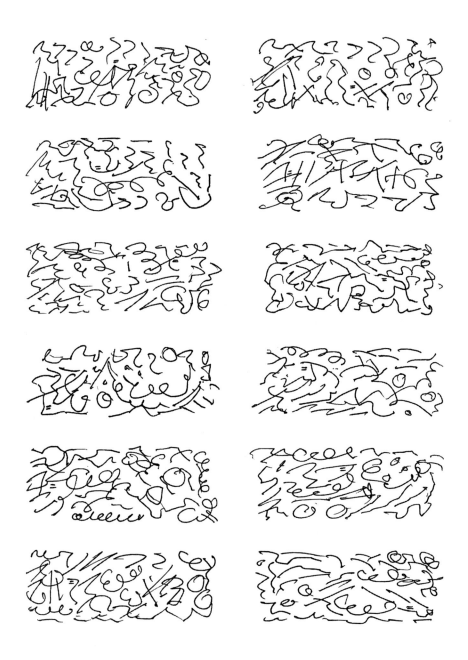

POTION FOR PLUG MAGIC

Mix only:

Olive oil
Molasses
Honey
Chewing gum
Yellow Magic potion
Quick Magic potion

Explanation of the Potion's Uses, Ingredients and Preparation

Plug Magic is for when you are stuck.

Mix and then bury it in your yard right away please.
Do not store this at all. Thank you.

POTION 10: POTION FOR SUCCESS MAGIC

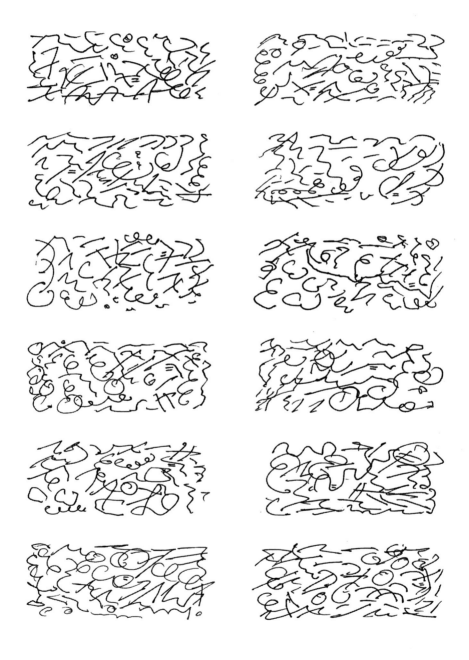

POTION FOR SUCCESS MAGIC

Mix and boil together:

Yellow Magic potion
Green Magic potion
Pink Magic potion
Coconut milk

Explanation of the Potion's Uses, Ingredients and Preparation

Success Magic is for when you are ready for success of your person or something else.

After you mix this one, please put it in a dish and place it in your kitchen, near your cooking space for up to 10 days.

POTION 11: POTION FOR DREAM MAGIC

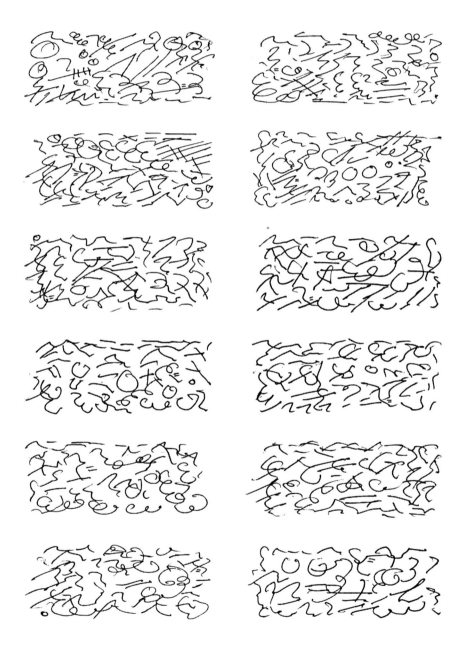

POTION FOR DREAM MAGIC

Mix only:

Olive oil
Coconut milk
Blueberry juice
Lavender oil

Explanation of the Potion's Uses, Ingredients and Preparation

Dream Magic is for when you like a type of dream. You will need to remember what to say when you are finished mixing. (*I asked whether she meant that at the end of mixing the potion, one needed to announce what type of dream it will bring. She answered, "Yes, please, please, Miss!"*)

This works very well alone and also with Purple Magic.

After you have mixed this and you have said what kind of dream you like, place in a bowl beside your bed.

Do not keep this for longer than a day.

POTION 12: POTION FOR 3H MAGIC

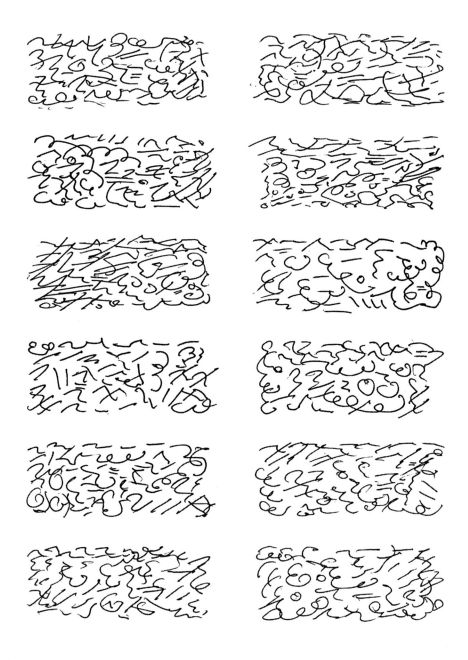

POTION FOR 3H MAGIC

Mix only:

Olive oil
Chili powder
Poppy seeds
Paper ashes

Explanation of the Potion's Uses, Ingredients and Preparation

3H Magic is for when you would like to make something three times hotter.

When you are mixing, please remember to think of what you want hotter. Then place the potion in a dish and we will eat it. If you wouldn't mind, please leave a glass of water beside the dish because it will be hot on our tongues.

Do not keep this longer than a day.

POTION 13: POTION FOR COLD MAGIC

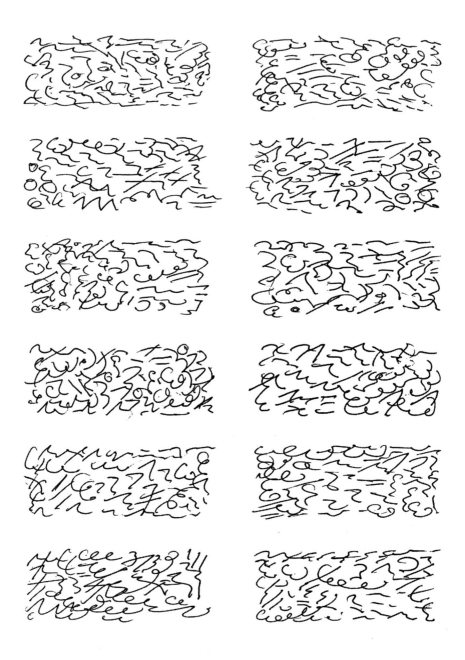

POTION FOR COLD MAGIC

Mix together and place in the freezer (or put in the snow):

Water
Banana peel
Pine needles
Oak bark

Explanation of the Potion's Uses, Ingredients and Preparation

Cold Magic is for when you would like to freeze something in your life — only if you like it.

You do not need to mix a lot of this; but when you are done mixing, put it in a dish in your freezer or you can put it in the snow for 30 days. (*I asked whether one should put a written piece of paper in the mixture before freezing, stating what one wanted to freeze. The answer: "Think of it as you stir the mixture with your spoon."*)

POTION 14: POTION FOR YELLOW EYES MAGIC

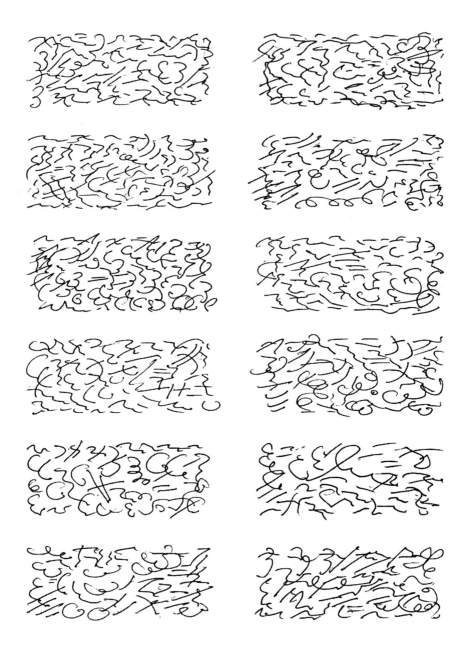

POTION FOR YELLOW EYES MAGIC

Mix together and boil:

Olive oil
Peppermint oil
White cat fur
Flour

Explanation of the Potion's Uses, Ingredients and Preparation

Yellow Eyes Magic is for when you would like to see very beautiful sights. This is an easy one, but please use scissors to cut your cat's fur because if you yank on it he will get mad, then you will be in trouble. Also, please ask him if it's OK so you are not rude.

This should be placed in a bowl on the floor, but watch out so your cat doesn't eat it. You can keep it there for 10 days.

POTION 15: POTION FOR RED HAND MAGIC

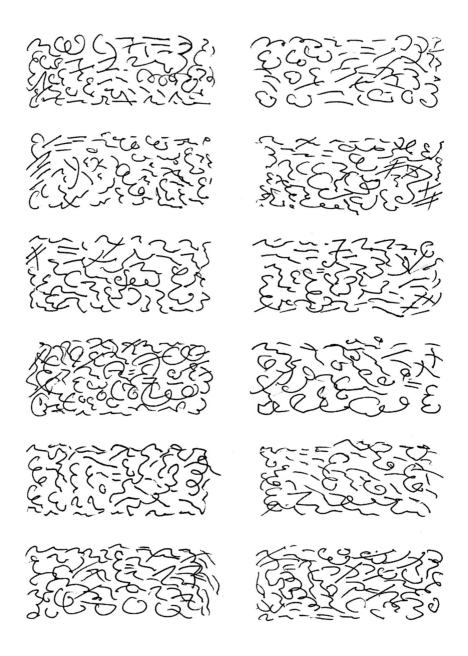

POTION FOR RED HAND MAGIC

Mix and boil:

Olive oil
Oregano oil
Chili powder
Raspberry juice
Bendover oil

Explanation of the Potion's Uses, Ingredients and Preparation

Red Hand Magic is for when you feel your friend is being sneaky and you would like to know the truth.

When you have finished mixing this, put some in your friend's garden. You can store this for 10 days inside your icebox.

Earth's Water-Fairies Get Their Wings

As the fairies from Venus, and the two groups from Lyra, poured into various areas on Earth, the oceans became very congested. I received the following communication from one of the Earth's water fairies, asking that I get help from Mother:

"I can't talk to you today because your hair is too dry.[19] I am stuck here in the ocean and my friends are here too. Could you please not leave us out? Please, please, do not forget to remember us. The rainy day will be very sad. But also please remember, we need some feet to walk on."

After this was brought to Mother's attention, all Earth's former water-fairies were given feet and wings, giving them the ability to make their way to the valley of fairies. The water-fairies from Venus and Lyra remained in the oceans.

19 My hair is "dry" because I am on dry land.

Part Five

The Magic of the Fairies from the Pleiades

Seven Secrets from the Pleiades

On the 16th of November, 28,000 fairies, elves, and other fairy-like beings arrived on Earth from the Pleiades, bringing another jewel for Mother's crown.

The following seven secrets were given to me by the two fairies: Aaaashviishmaaashooeesh and Miichshaaooeevaaoom.

SECRET ONE

You thought the Earth in Antares began.
Partially true, but you misunderstand.
The Earth was by Mother firstly formed
In beauty arrayed, magnificently adorned.

Seven star-systems around her lay
Of each she was part, one could rightly say.
Each held a chakra like a colored lens
Reflecting their light like a precious gem.

As the light shone, fueled by Her love
More stars formed below and above.

The Earth is thus the ancient one
It was from here that life had begun.

She was larger than this Earth that we see;
She was larger by far, in fact times three.
As Tiamat, or Eternal Mother, was she known,
Also because she was the Goddess's home.

But then began an awful age
Of separation, and a descension phase,
When Kings decided to dominate,
Light distorted, and the planets pushed away.

In that age of opposite light repelled
They could not stay, as you can tell.
The chakras they carried, sacred and true
Were carried with them and flew away too.

Mother removed from these centers of light
The codes of creation, and sealed them tight
In the heart of a gem hidden within each of the star-systems.
And now begins their sacred return,
By those who have earned by guarding these gems, the right to
return.

Fairies they are who kept them safe
The ones who are gathering in the hidden place;
Now unify the chakras into one
The reign of the Goddess has begun.

SECRET TWO

All the fairies gathered here
Once were from Earth, it must be clear.

And now a secret must be told:
In previous cycles, when chakras unfurled
In a specific order, creation occurred.
Thus when they left, it happened too,
In a certain order to de-structure too.

But that which unraveled must now come home.
In a special order each chakra's tone
Must play the new creational tune
And when it does there will be a boom.

SECRET THREE

A big bang will happen and creation occur
Spread far and wide; but some must return.
Same energy attracts, you must understand,
We now have the same energy as those chakras did have.
They will come back to take their place
Around the Earth and Mother's grace.

SECRET FOUR

After the expansion and creation is done,
A long time of rest will be most welcome.
Fifty-nine thousand years will then begin,
That we shall have peace and grow within.

The time-period given is in our time,
As though the moments walked in a line,
To focus on details, infrastructures build,
To explore ourselves and what makes us fulfilled.

SECRET FIVE

The chakras have energy of those who'll come back
But though it is strong, there is something it lacks.
The gemstones, too, have taken it on
And though it attracts, it would take too long.
And so another way must be found
As they hasten away, to turn them around.

SECRET SIX

Thus Mother has planned to create a bond;
A bond of love, for of children we're fond.
Thus the children are sired by those not from here,
Two from Antares already are here.

And so on the night we return to Earth,
Three come to father; and then comes a fourth
The two that are here and twenty more
Create a strong bond, much more than before.

The fathers chosen, of all most aware,
Will want to be here because they care.
The offspring will grow – a bridge between worlds
And with their birth star systems turn.

SECRET SEVEN

With their birth, comes a wondrous gift,
Five more chakras in the cosmos birthed.
Five star-systems more gather around
The Earth is aglow, new stars in the heavens are found.

Pleiadean Fairy Meanings

It can be seen from the meanings given by Mother to the 40 Pleiadean Fairies listed below just how powerful they must be. The areas of life they will oversee, instructing multitudes of fairies in their duties, are of a magnitude normally reserved for angels or lords.

It is also of immense value to know the names and meanings of such powerful fairies in order to call for assistance in these specified areas of life. Establishing a friendly relationship with them will enhance our chances of significant assistance from them; fairies are very loyal to friendship. These meanings give us an indication as to the kinds of roles that the Pleiadean fairies will play now that they have come to Earth (see also Appendix II, "400 Fairies from the Pleiades").

40 PLEIADEAN FAIRIES AND THEIR MEANINGS

1. **Suuleevaumbiishlaamishvaauum**: He who oversees the legions of fairies who clean up the earth.
2. **Petelmiishpixeeemaaumbiiish**: He who oversees legions to change old ways of hardship to new ways of effortless joy.
3. **Twirlabaalameriibaaaladuum**: He who oversees legions to transform fatigue into energy.

4. **Viishlaaaevershmaalaavoom**: She who oversees legions to bring delight, comfort and companionship to children and babies.
5. **Preevaaanaamasunamaalalaalaaa**: He who oversees legions to erase old limiting expectations and replace it with hope, trust, adventure and inspiration.
6. **Veemaaaooshteuumehvaaadaanaveh**: She who oversees legions to renew the earth's eco-systems into perfect balance.
7. **Tuuleeevaaumpaapaduumdeedee**: She who oversees the development of new plant life to bring beauty and life to all areas on earth.
8. **Veriiveeridaaoomgeeaaoom**: He who oversees legions to guard the integrity and condition of the polar caps.
9. **Leedlhemmdaavaammuudaaa**: She who oversees legions to comfort dying animals.
10. **Silvaanaanaekvaaoommaah**: She who oversees legions to change patterns and expectations of hardship during childbirth into joy and beauty.
11. **Baaariichnkorsiilaamtonaashiireema**: She who oversees legions to prevent distortion in the media, arts education or literature from registering in the minds and hearts of all.
12. **Borshiimanoorkaaa**: She who oversees legions to replace distortion in art, media, education, literature with inspiration and enlightenment.
13. **Simiishnariichvaasumneshborlaaanakiimnaabushvishna-simkalarenomervsalish**: She who oversees legions to inspire artists, educators, journalists, and politicians to lead responsibly, impeccably, and inspirationally.
14. **Cantaleemavishna**: She who oversees legions to reveal potential, new opportunities and moments of chance to all, bringing confidence in their own discernment and decisions.

15. **Bolasaqvisaabiivaaaraanasiilavushnishmaaraa**: He who oversees legions to enhance humans' physical abilities and the restoration of youth, vitality and strength to bodies.
16. **Kantishvaaasiiilaanaaamoyishvanishkasaaa**: He who oversees legions to promote understanding, empathy and assimilative listening, and communication between species, groups, individuals, and with nature.
17. **Burnaalaaakaaasiimoonapelaaasaavtiikotaa**: She who oversees legions to support, delight and enhance the joy of Mother and all those who live in her palace.
18. **Siiikoooraaalamiishnaakiishraasaaavasiitol**: She who oversees legions to create magical beauty in women everywhere.
19. **Biishkoolariishvapeeshkaciiibaaaatasoupiraaalaaa**: He who oversees legions for dissolution of injurious thoughts and the prevention of their being acted out.
20. **Aaalamaaaranakiishpataalaruumsaaanaaa**: He who oversees legions to remove any toxicity and obesity from the bodies of humanity.
21. **Kaysoooraaasatiiivaniimsaaalaanaaaap**: She who oversees legions to remove dependency on medication and substances for well-being.
22. **Aaaashviishmaashooeeshmiichshaaooeevaaoom**: She who oversees legions to stimulate the 12 pairs of emotions in all beings in areas where needed.
23. **Mooshaaaooeevoshaarma**: He who oversees legions to bring child abuse perpetrators to immediate exposure and justice, to heal and remove innocents from such abuse.
24. **Oomasesheeaaosesheeaomeshcheeaao**: He who oversees legions to convert industry, consumer products and urban and farming practices to being more environmentally friendly.

25. **Mesheeaaaooeemauooeshee**: She who orchestrates legions bringing serendipitous and joyous surprises, unexpected gifts and abundance and answers to prayers.

26. **Shemsehaaooaaeemeshemooaaee**: She who oversees legions in healing loneliness by establishing a joyous and balanced relationship with self, and nature, by inspiring romance with life and bringing the right friends and partners together.

27. **Meshemwaaooeeaameshemooee**: She who oversees legions in tempering and balancing climatic conditions for optimum enjoyment, growth and ability to flourish.

28. **Shemsheeaamoesheeaaooeshemshemaaooeshem**: She who oversees the stimulation of the senses, the appreciation of beauty and life's experience and an awareness of others' divinity.

29. **Ooaashemaaooeshemaaooeshemaaooeshemaa**: She who oversees legions stimulating the awareness necessary to feel constant and deep love, praise and gratitude.

30. **Vishaaemaaooeshemaashemooaaeshemaaesh**: She who oversees legions promoting visions and inner knowing and love for and about Mother as the One Being in which all life dwells and has its being.

31. **Maashemaashwaaeshemaaooaashemwashemwaashemaaa**: She who oversees legions to bring conflict resolution through innovation and clear perception.

32. **Esheemwaaooshaameshemwaooshemaashemwemaashem-waa**: : He who promotes through legions vegetarianism and harmlessness towards animals and other life-forms.

33. **Eeeshemwaaoooeshemwaaaooeshemwaaoooshemwa**: She who oversees legions to promote joy of labor, accountability, self-responsibility and a desire for excellence in the results of labor, as well as self-sufficiency and a sense of accomplishment.

34. **Aaahnaaaseshwaaaooosheshemwaaaoooeshemwaaooshem-ooowa**: She who oversees legions to promote balance between rest and activity, an appreciation for silence, joy in balanced aloneness and inactivity, as well as silence of the mind.

35. **Eeshemwaeeshmaawaaseeshemwaaoosheemaaaa**: She who oversees legions encouraging self-knowledge, self-respect, self-love, self-worth and self-exploration.

36. **Ooshaashaawaashemaawooshaashemeshwaaaaooshemva**: She who oversees legions encouraging absolute truth in all areas of life, including judiciously speaking heart-felt feelings and desires.

37. **Ooshemwaasaameshaoooshaamaashaasheshmaaoooeee-maaaa**: She who restores through legions the respect and understanding of the feminine, the masculine, the aged and the young.

38. **Aameshwaseshmasheshoomaaooeshmaoooshesh**: She who oversees legions who inspire the creation of -- and create through magic -- inspirational, exquisite, life-enhancing habitats, living and working spaces and educational environments for all.

39. **Aaamaaeshooaamaeshmaashaamaseshmaaoshmaa**: She who through legions assists in parenting, teaching, comforting and loving orphans and homeless children, inspiring parents to want to love and adopt them.

40. **Ooomaasheemaaasheshmaaoshmaasheshmaaneshmashesh-maooaaa**: She who through legions of fairies fulfills the Mother's bidding, desires, needs, and finds ways in which to bring delight to Her.

Part Six

The Magic of the Fairies from Andromeda and Arcturus

Introduction to the Candles of Wisdom, called "Prehina"

The Andromedan "Six Candles of Wisdom" were not received directly from the Andromedan fairies who arrived on the 17th November; instead, we received them from the Holy Mother of all Creation.[20] The reasons for this are as follows:

- On November 16, the day before their arrival on Earth, the Andromedan fairies gave all their secrets or wisdom away to the cosmos and the other fairies. They therefore had no more secrets to give.
- The reason they did this is that the Andromedan fairies, like the Arcturian fairies who arrived the same day, have the philosophy that if you give someone something, you have to give everything; in other words, they give "all or nothing". The Andromedan fairies chose to give away all their secrets, as well as their magic, which they placed in the gemstone they were returning for Mother's crown.
- The Six Candles, or secrets, were received from Mother on the 17th November, 2006.

---

20 Anything spoken in Her language is magic in and of itself, in that it manifests as spoken.

• That night, Mother gave the Andromedan fairies their magic back. For that reason, we were able to photograph the tiny fairies, who were so small that angels had to carry them to Earth (otherwise it would have taken them 300 years to reach here on their own).

"Prehina"
("Six Candles" in Andromedan Fairy Language)

The Prehina gift from the fairies of Andromeda (received by us from Mother), is a series of illuminating secrets in six areas of life: music, play, work, magic, children and family groups. The following candles are written in Mother's language.

CANDLE ONE: THE SECRETS OF MUSIC

Secret 1

Vils klanach ve rush, u trua virhat
Spelech vi blush, uretvi visach
Belesh bliva urvahet bivarit
Elesh mi saverhet nun spaverhit

No clocks there are, nor time[21], nor space
But frequency changes mark the pace
Every hour it changes. Twelve times this is so
It then repeats; and like before it goes

Mech priha verushvi skalet uvervaa
Belech vi asvarv herut velespaa

---

21 There is no word in Mother's language for "time".

Krenuch mi staber herut elestu
Belsh ikvanaver herut milveshtu

For music you play or the songs that you sing
To enhance your life and joy to bring
Trace the songs of birds all day long
How each hour they change the tones of their song

Besh aber var hech sutra va ura
Belesh pra-ut savar velsh averstra
Kels mich pauret velskatel urit
Kruag mi nanastru urech valabit

Then emulate them and the change that occurs
The right music at the right time emotions will stir
Sound is a clock, frequency is time
Learn this secret and power is thine

Secret 2

Versh echva urusvi keles vrivar
Spel uvra huch spavi ulech spar
Nun spesbi klesh avri uvravar

Color is tone made visible to see
If you play in the forest too much of the green
The soul will feel that excess has been

Branuch veles nustrava heres tra u vat
Shpi uvra uvresbi herut sar vu tat
Belanoch verklut uravespi strahur
Keles vi nuch vravi tre usbanaklur

In the forest play the tones that are red
By yellow or blue too, the soul will be fed
In deserts of course the green will be fine
Each climatic region has its own music sublime

Secret 3

Kruavestri paruch minuvestri baha
Pluanuchvi uvavrastu, pelesh vraha
Sutl achvranastuk elechbi stra-uhet
Peleshvi manabrut upelsbi straunet

Where tones are missing, illusion abides
Sound distorted, illusion of illness resides
Through music these tones can be fully restored
The missing tones once more can be yours

Vera biskirat utra selvi shpat
Pelech vi bru utra vis abruspat
Helech inor sabu helspi varanech
Eres vi isbavar struvet manuret

But now as you know, each time of day
A tone reigns supreme, so find when to play
The tone that you need, the flaw to heal
The sounds will restore and better you'll feel

Secret 4

Versh vrasna uber fat heles par vi
Klech esh bra uversat hels bravari
Plech plaa uhurs tre a varavi
Skeluch paruf us va ba tra u vi

Twelve notes there are in the scale that you know
Each note promotes an emotion's flow
Twelve pairs there are of emotions true[22]
The key of the music will choose one for you

Verskrachva urish manuhetvi sklauraa
Versatva uvish treuach manuraa
Pulunuchvi plaret uresvi pelaa
Varu helvink uskach ururaa

Emotions must pulse, the two in each pair
In the same way the music must pulse here and there
Proactive at times, then receptive again
The male and the female this represents.

Belech struavi vaa heshpi kleraa
Strua varvit ulech bi klarit

When frequencies pulse, awareness will raise
Your life will become a song of praise[23]

22 See Appendix for the 12 pairs of emotions. See detailed description in *The Ring of Truth*
23 *The Ring of Truth* explains the relationship between praise and awareness

CANDLE TWO: THE SECRETS OF PLAY

Secret 1

Varshvi sklurechba ulesbi varhaa
Pret priu nanavish uklechva baraa
Pelesnu haresvaa uruklechbi strauvaa
Vruspret unesbi ulech klauraa

Play is active, it is often thought
But the other half of play must be sought
As in all things, balance must be
For play to deliver its gifts to thee

Gelech shtra u vespi blauch strauhaa
Tru bela vechspi uret beleshtraa
Minur sarvu geleshva uret palanich
Streu bra velespaa klet branavich

Play must be active and passive as well
Comprehend this and then its secrets I'll tell
For play the blockages of mind will release
Emotions, too, it will set free.

Secret 2

Kranish his pelech vu
Arnu belsh blich manastru
Kel vi vaa u vilistraa hik
Belu peleshtru na ur blavik

Is it that you wish to excel?
Then I exhort you to listen well

Play will help your accomplishments grow
For one promotes the other you know.

Kelus vistra velus es
Ninhur barkla varlu plesh
Brisk bra krut u nanuvirt
Elch u vastraa mil planirt

The harder you play, the more you achieve
Where the other is not, the one cannot be.

Secret 3

Estra heshu velech nut
Asvru belstru stranik blut
Pelesh vi ustrachbi haa
Klut ma sutvaa verestraa

The wee folk want assistance from you
If you will help, here's what to do
Plants will grow wherever you play
But be consistent and play each day.

Peshvis belechvi hares tra uni
Birs bra uvravespi ulech pranabi
Kelsut manurim ura vespi trahaa
Elech vra nutvi klash uvrabaa

Nature withers when ambition is blind
When work and strife is all we can find
The desire to revel must go hand in hand

Inner balance inevitably leads to restoring balance throughout the land.

Secret 4

Bra brush branu vespi ulech minaru
Belesh vivaspra, uret klanavu
Kreshbi uvra spuch u vra vespi aruk
Nun spelvi achvra sut hel sut velvravuk

To understand concepts, relationships see
To see them, you first must cognizant be
Of maps of space, of which there are two
One is within, and one outside you.

Kirshaber verut urna vechspi verhat
Klush aber hurvavet urs varuspach
Nun stelbi u lachvra urhespi verluch
Spi ura vilstravaa uklech varna bruch.

These maps are formed at the age of five
No sooner nor later, however hard you strive
These maps are formed in children through play
Through running and jumping and playing each day.

Velskla ubrahupspi urech tra-uni
Velupshpa kreruspravi speluch varuni

Without these maps their letters aren't right
Play therefore helps them to read and to write

CANDLE THREE: THE SECRETS OF WORK

Secret 1

Barsklu hirs vir klaravi urech sparaklu
Brish ubra hestruvi minach varaklu
Bel astra-uvach spirabich klauret
Min hurs u strauvat kleru baru-set

First it builds up, then it tears down,
For it is based on a concept profound
That all that goes out, must also come in
Everything pulses without and within.

Kelefba hurukvi spela hur varsit
Kels us vra achvrabi ules balastrit
Mish pres usvraresbi klunisvra varha
Vel pris pra evreshbi klech uvrastat

After twelve hours of work that you've done
A time of de-structuring must be begun
If not, the work you have done falls apart,
Then decay in the cells of your body will start.

Fru vit uvra lechspi minur klabusat
Velech pra-uvrabi hel ush varstat

Be therefore wise and work not too hard
And thus it shall be that you will go far.

Secret 2

Kerslu ech vra sut nit het valasbi
Erch klu achvra kru varasbi
Klesh nit alsva ech vrabit
Klusva hechbi stalach nit

When work isn't fueled by the joy of your heart
It can't to the cosmos benefit impart
It needs emotion pure and true
To ripple through all and return to you.

Gir stra urechbi hirut paruve
Mish klia struavet belech klaruve

A loveless task brings lack your way
A spiral that's inward must bring decay.

Varstra minuhet ula vech bileshtra
Vilichpe uruf paresh mishtra vilesta
Kruag ur nuf parvu klulech brich brasta
Mirnug ules varasbi sparuch veleshtra

Filled with love for the work you do
The benefits spiral away from you
Causing increase wherever it goes
Like a life-giving river its blessings will grow.

Secret 3

Krech staber uretvi herush barnustach
Viles ba krugelva nur bish plavach

Sterut steura urnavesh pla-ura
Veluchva urishpravi kleru vanusta

What doesn't go forth through the cosmos to bless
Does not produce results that are best
For increase can't come to work that is done
To the self-centered benefit of only one.

Secret 4

Virsh na drua velsklat uvefri barklut
Hilch treva helsat ubravechspri barut
Milklish vil es rutvaba sklura harnestu
Ules viachvraba erus stanavuch

The clothes that you wear, the food you eat
Must be made with love or they're incomplete
When there's a hole in the web of life,
Something withheld, one must pay the price

Kraug minerva klaug starech
Elsh planu vanabi brish brach varech

Energy therefore is taken away
From the user of products made in this way.

CANDLE FOUR: THE SECRETS OF MAGIC

Secret 1

Virskra uvravechspi urlut veleskra
Mish tre uvra heresvi erlut mishpata

Klesut vilva velesbi klarut minarech
Starok uvra velespi klasut virnastech

How long, do you say, will it take to appear
As I do the magic you've given me here
Three things it takes to successfully do
The magical spells we have given to you.

Preshaber verut usterva barut
Pelesh vi nutvi uklet banasut
Perch nis vis uklat vraber usutvi vrabu
Elesh vi nut vrabit urech ustrabu

The three ingredients to successful spells:
Love, joy and energy work very well
Neutral, negative and positive aspects are they
Important are they in the part they play.

Barach vi nut uluhelshbi sklaru
Kel ufvra vishpavi urech manaru
Sul mish pliklat uretvi miret
Pres uver ushvraba ures manavet

Each has a role in the magic you do
From the fairies comes this message to you:
Blame not the spell if it should elude you
For you need these three keys the spells to do.

Secret 2

Pelesh vi staber elechvra urahet
Vistra us aver nuret manarut

Pelesh vru verestra uchvi vra starom
Kru mich palesh vavi unich vil stalom

Love will hasten the effects that you want
Thus love what you do, that which will come
Love these secrets that have come from so far
Love one another and whomever you are.

Secret 3

Granuch veresh hers parvaa
Kru nutvi steruk belch us vas branutaa
Kelsh shtra uvra uter brish brak hernavu
Klusat uvra bers krauta heruk kresnavu

In doing magic, building blocks you'll need
Joy attracts them; pulls them in with speed
The raw material from which to produce
Is the cosmic life-force for you to use.

Bilch vra nutvi staus vilsh achvra staruk
Erus bra skruvrabi helsut manavuk

Joy is negative and thus can receive
The elements to build what you conceive.

Secret 4

Gluchfrak banasut mileshpa trahut kelesvaa
Prufbak urespavi belich venestraa
Berechpaa uhustravi klesh us va us baktaa
Mir pla urespavi klusut menestaa

Energy comes in three forms[24] as you know
One is a ray of light, the other the force that moves;
The one we mean is an element, one of creation's needs
Permeates everything, everywhere, residing all around thee.

Kulushbri u brech va brut
Stelech a u-vra banasut
Peleshviplaa ureshbi varuch
Stelech pri vaa uvanabruch

Like a sponge, and through your skin
Energy without, draw within
Absorb as much as you can stand
Then raise it up to the pineal gland

Ku ulu steavit blish blech parvaa
Krechnut stu avravit uhursh u starvaa
Nin skel banasut uvra vespi varspet
Skle hur uvra vanashet klu ut hurspavet

Raise it up like with a drinking straw
Suck in your breath, as up you draw
The energy into the center of your head
Hold it there as your spell is said.

Bra bis klanuvar uru asba sta-arut
Krechna uvravar uruesbi banaklut
Elech prenusva uklesh vanabik
Stelsut uvra vaspava uret manablik
Greknach velhispi urech vanabel
Eras vernukvi sparuch eskradel

24 See "What is Energy" in *The Ring of Truth*

But how to release that which you hold
Listen well as the secret is told
Like a sponge that you squeeze, muscles contract
Deep in the head with your eyes tilted back
Pour it into the spell you have said
Releasing energy from inside your head.

CANDLE FIVE: THE SECRETS OF CHILDREN

Secret 1

Gruchsta bileshbi stanarok verskraurit
Bil bech vra uvresbi bla-uch stanarik
Grubilshpa urechbi veluskra virskravi
Belshpa va uvravik urech spanavi

That which once was, now has been changed
It only is fair that gifts are exchanged
Formerly children took perception at birth
Took away from their parents that which was theirs.

Krustra bilech spara elechsva uhurutvi klanaruk
Trehur pa ulesva uhur vanastik
Pelva uhusvri urechspi elesva
Ru-setvi u keleshva u ret banastik

With each child, a little light lost
Thus the children came at a cost
But now this is changed, light is now gained
And so for each child the parent is paid.

Secret 2

Bruestrava klu-uhespri brech treuna varablit
Kluesh upriviva urech strauvit
Kelesh vi nutvi varuech ustravaa
Glu-uvra hechspavi uset varivaa

Written in the Book of Life; the following has been said:
Parents no longer lock children into belief systems that are dead
No longer are assemblage points fixed after birth[25]
Setting free the children of planets like Earth.

Secret 3

Kelshtru vitva kla avuhet
Mishtra hutvi erch vanabet
Klesvaa struanach brusba avruvaa
Berchva husbi kles u avruhaa

Because the assemblage point is not locked anymore
The children can see far more than before
Into realms unknown they will freely gaze
With sights to delight and bring joy their way.

Barechpi unesh varuvis uspalvi
Krech aver sutravat shpaluch ushstabi

No longer does aught exist that could make them afraid
And thus now this gift is brought to our babes.

---

25 Assemblage point is a ball of light on the edge of the fields around the bodies or fields of man. (Explained in *Secrets of the Hidden Realms*)

Secret 4

Gel aver veruchspi klanuber versat
Pelachva uhesvrafat staruch varabi
Plesh rut uravespi erech tranavu
Ubla va spechvabi ures trana du

Four minutes after birth - once prison bars made
Before, those that touched programmed the babes
Giving beliefs, even though seldom right
That colored the vision of the child's whole life.

Glanuch starechvi urstru urarat
Pelsh bich vel uvrava uhur avrustak
Pel nuchvi veles vra vaa speluch vilanut
Hersh pri u ech vrabi uher aversut

But now the child, during this crucial time
Bestows upon others vision sublime
Those that touch will now receive
Innocent vision and faith to believe.

CANDLE SIX: THE SECRETS OF FAMILY GROUPS

Secret 1

Vra ma vit hesh traug vi nach
Pelsh ubrav uret vis ba vach
Truag manur uluvesbi trahaa
Kelesh vi tra ma nug vis u bataa

Previously chosen based on that which opposed
Families often did not feel like home.
Opposite energies much friction brought
Through discomforts were the lessons taught.

Skel achva ureshpi kelustru mispataa
Vis usbavespi ukluch veleshtraa
Baruk nin hur set vravi ulechbi strauhaa
Stel uvra veshpavi uklech vish bavaa

But growth now comes through support
Through loving examples learning is brought
Families now are chosen this way:
When energy is the same, together they'll stay.

Secret 2

Bri-esh tra u-va ulavechspi travu
Klesh bra-u vespavi kluach manatu
Bel hik us bavaa minestra stravaa
Kelush bri uch vrabi stel us vasbaa

Decreed it has been by Mother's own voice
That those drawn close, come by energy's choice[26]
But because all are turning to light, understand well
While like ones are attracted, some distance is held.

Glistrekvi kranech uhus pelesnur
Klanu vi bres tra u vavrablur
Stel huf ufbra uchvi stelelut beleshtur
Kla u vra vespavi veluch manestur

26 Recent cosmic changes have same energies attracting, but same light repelling. To keep
lightbeings from repelling one another, Mother decreed that heart energy should always slightly
exceed each person's light quotient.)

This will erase co-dependency's bane
We will love, but without neediness and pain
Inter-dependency offers support that we need
Balance and strength our sustenance will be.

Secret 3

Velshpri urech parave ulavek
Steru urat vravi kle-ug nanivuk
Blesh bli uvra vechspi ura heruvit
Kelesh vi uchvrava ures vanabit

At the birth of a child both parents rejoice
Both want to be with the baby by choice
Instinct is strong to support mother and child
The father delights to be by their side.

Stravink helsvra sutbravi elles tra uravech
Hersut bel uchstrabi uret manavech
Lu stravik elsh nut trava uklet viles ves
Uch miu strek vravi uret vana bes

Thus for a time in the life of a babe
New life supported and dependency reigns
As the baby grows bigger, tries things on his own
Father and mother teach by example shown.

Pleug ustra milleshpa nurhut vilstravaa
Kleug vla ustravi herut varestraa
Ma pri-eg ulvesbi kliu vanastat
Bilch ples u verarut u nes viushtat

Co-dependence though to independence turns
As the older child now on his own must learn
And as he sets forth to make his own home
Inter-dependence shows he is not all alone.

Veraski vivach utrechbi speraa
Belesh vi blich us tru vereraa
Pluach varavich uvra struvra verhaa
Varnech vrablik ures pre va haa

Secret 4

We ask now a question to see if you know
What happens when to pregnant mothers you show
Support and assistance in her time of need
If you don't know, then please give heed:

Klunech stri stravek ureshbi klauraa
Strechva vra blik usut varuhaa
Ninubirsh staurechbi kleuvas stauraa
Minuvech stau vesbi u klet stararaa

That which you shelter and offer to help
Is actually a gift you give to yourself.
The blessing you get, rejuvenation by name,
In the measure you give, that you will gain.

Pilistur klava vra u vech parlaa
Spispa varet uresh klu a vaa
And now end the candles of wisdom we give
May they bring wisdom to the way that you live.

The "Clean-up" Fairies of Andromeda

Over the eons of evolving separately, the various fairy groups from different planetary systems had developed different areas of expertise, as they had begun to focus more and more on specific tasks.

The fairies from Andromeda had become experts in the transmutation and elimination of all that no longer serves. In other words, they were the "clean-up crew". Having performed that function for ages, their assignments on Earth will mirror what they are used to doing. Again, it is of great value to be able to call on these fairies by name, if you are in need of help in any of these areas (see also Appendix III, "100 Angels from Andromeda" and Appendix IV, "100 Fairies from Andromeda").

1. **Bilibitspelspa**: The one who fills buildings with life supporting energy
2. **Ritlbispadin**: The one who removes all foul odors
3. **Drugelprinspa**: The one who ensures there is no pollution from vehicles nor building power/heat/cooling systems
4. **Gelspikstvapa**: The one who removes toxins and any harmful ingredients from all food
5. **Kluspekvispa**: The one who removes pollution and toxins from all water
6. **Kelidindlva**: The one who ensures that all development is sustainable and non-destructive
7. **Spenkeldistrava**: The one who cleans litter and garbage from roads, parks, recreational areas, oceans and deserts
8. **Vindelivaverna**: The one who cleans and filters impurities in the air we breathe and water we drink, wash, and swim in
9. **Pelivispadrna**: The one who cleans, disposes of and recycles human, animal, fish, and bird waste

10. **Estrikelvisprna**: The one who purifies water in all oceans, seas, lakes, rivers, lagoons and ponds
11. **Vendondikna**: The one who ensures there is no violence towards any living being
12. **Kendlviskpapra**: The one who cleans and purifies written words yet allows artistic expression
13. **Jeshnyekevraoshemkavya**: The one who purifies depressed thoughts
14. **Eshnauviicarvicareshnau**: The one who removes trauma from children
15. **Yevenshenraeshamkevye**: The one who removes trauma from animals
16. **Eeshamajioshemkavya**: The one who ensures that all education is of the highest knowledge and wisdom
17. **Iishemoshemanyakavya**: The one who removes toxins from all lands
18. **Eshnomenkoshishaparna**: The one who ensures that people do not destroy property
19. **Viieshplenkoshishkarvaka**: The one who washes lenses on cameras
20. **Exploneshkaexplavicta**: The one who launders soiled clothing
21. **Evyeshenkoeshmarkenyo**: The one who washes little fairy hands
22. **Evshevtuliespanvira**: The one who washes dirty dishes
23. **Eshpukenshaeshpuvarna**: The one who washes leaves on trees
24. **Leshkuplenkavishawina**: The one who washes car windows
25. **Wieshplenyaeshkamvila**: The one who cleans environmental waste
26. **Ishplakartaeshnarvishna**: The one who cleans radiation pollution

27. **Eshuplenkareshnarvishua:** The one who ensures that all crops and foods are pure, safe, and beneficial to eat

28. **Vishuaplenkarplenkarvishnar:** The one who ensures all TV, radio, and movies are pure and unpolluted

29. **Eshtuplenktunarsharvishtu:** The one who ensures that people do not steal

30. **Viiesharnauviiveshvarna:** The one who ensures that all energy sources are non-polluting

31. **Eshkuplenkarvishnaparta:** The one who cleans all animals and nature (rain forests, etc.)

32. **Vishnapartawvishnakeshvar:** The one who dissolves psychic impressions

33. **Keshnarplenkarvishnapurtam:** the one who ensures that all sexuality is respectful, consensual, and pure

34. **Krishnapurnowkrishnaparvau:** the one who removes pollution and toxins from all air

35. **Vieshvecnowviieshvarnau:** the one who cleans all air particles

36. **Ekeshvishnauvishesharnau:** the one who cleans gaseous fumes

37. **Semshemvishnauvishnauvarta:** the one who cleans modern equipment

38. **Varnaukemshaueshsemvisha:** the one who removes impure thoughts from all minds and impure feelings from all hearts

39. **Kripulinslaprnana:** the one who cleans up garbage dumps and toxic waste

40. **Kenarvitavieshplenshar:** the one who clears away discordant music and spreads a desire for harmonious and joyful music

The Fairies from Arcturus

The Arcturian fairies arrived on November 17, 2006. Like the Andromedan fairies, their philosophy is to give "all or nothing". They did not want to give only partial pieces of their magic; and insisted on giving *all* of it. As a separate book would be required to accommodate all of this, they are waiting "in the wings" for us to receive their information. For this reason, we weren't yet allowed to photograph them.

Part Seven

The New Fairy Calendar

The Fairy Calendar for All Fairies Now on Earth

The Fairy Calendar is new; it is a gift from Mother to synchronize all the groups of fairies on Earth. Time, as it was once known, has ceased to exist. Now, there is a succession of a series of frequencies that repeats itself over and over (see Figure 4, "The New Fairy Calendar").

In the case of the fairies, their day (a specific frequency) is 12.6 of "our minutes"[27]. To them it feels as long as a day currently does to us. There are 12 days in a week (their week to us is 2 hours 31.2 minutes long). Every one of their years consists of 3 of their weeks; so *to us* their year would be 7 hours and 33.6 minutes of *our time*. Their calendar maps out 9 of their years of frequency "days"; and after that it repeats itself. Their 9-year calendar is to us 2 days 20 hours and 2.4 minutes long; to them it is 324 days long.

---

27 It should be understood that we are referring to "our time" as a point of comparison; it is a reference to the illusion of time, with the sun appearing to rise and set each day.

A SUMMARY OF THE GROUPS OF FAIRIES THE CALENDAR REPRESENTS

Before the fairies started arriving in their various groups, Mother had already called the cosmic life-force center back from Antares. When the Fairies from Lyra came to Earth, the cosmic crown chakra followed; and when the Earth-Fairies from Lyra came, the cosmic chakra of the third eye followed.

The third group of fairies to arrive was from Venus, and the heart center of the cosmos followed them here. Then came the group from the Pleiades and with them, the cosmic third chakra followed. The Andromedan fairies were next, and the cosmic throat chakra followed.

All the groups mentioned brought with them their specific languages. A hundred squares on the calendar depict concepts in these languages. Each group brought a gem for Mother's crown that she had asked them to safeguard (with the exception of the life-force center on Antares). The codes of creation had been transferred from all other chakras into the gems guarded by the fairies.

The Arcturian fairies, as previously explained, are waiting to give "all" they have; but with their arrival on Earth, the second chakra of the cosmos followed. Those who hold the root chakra and the gem associated with it, I may not yet speak or write about, as "it is not for this book".

The Calendar Squares

Each fairy group has a "Birthday", the day when they were all created. With the exception of the Arcturians (who did not want to give their birthday or language for the calendar, nor partial pieces of magic) these birthdays are marked on the calendar as special days for great merriment and festivities.

The Birthdays (marked on the calendar as double squares) are as follows:

- Earth Fairies: Day 21
- Lyra Fairies: Day 34
- Earth-Fairies from Lyra: Day 55
- Venus Fairies: Day 89
- Pleiadean Fairies: Day 102
- Andromedan Fairies: Day 203

It is clear from this information that:

- The Earth Fairies were the first to be created; they have been alive the longest.
- The Earth-Fairies from Lyra were created later (perhaps for the special role they played in safeguarding the gems). Although the Earth-Fairies from Lyra retained the same language as the Earth Fairies, they are a newer group.

There are twelve blank squares on the calendar which are colored in purple. I am not aware of what these squares represent; it is possible that they won't be filled-in until the Arcturians release their information.

It is interesting to note that the mathematics of the fairies was different from the math used by humans on Earth. For example, in our math 3 X 12 = 36; whereas the fairies calculated it to be 34.6. On November 19th, Mother synchronized our two forms of mathematics, as one more step towards bringing our realms together.

THE NEW FAIRY CALENDAR

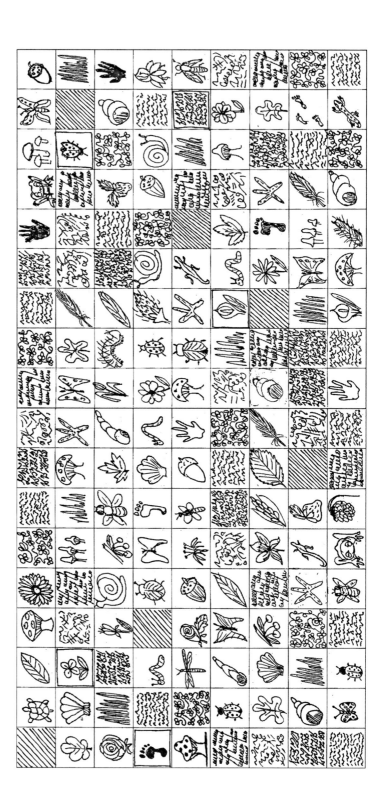

Figure 8

The Deeper Meaning of the Calendar

There is much hidden information to the Calendar that must be felt with the heart (see Figure 5, "The Key to the Fairy Calendar"). It was gently pointed out to me that it was "rude" to ask too many specifics as I prodded and probed for information. I did, however, receive the following explanations:

- The calendar is a portal to access fairies.
- The symbols are frequencies: The higher the frequency, the higher the fairies fly. For example, during a butterfly day, they may be 20 feet off the ground; and during a turtle day, 4 feet off the ground. They wouldn't give me further information on which symbol was for which frequency; but said if we could feel it with our heart, we would know where to look for them.

THE KEY TO THE FAIRY CALENDAR

1	2	3	4	5	6	7	8	9	10	11	12	13	14	15	16	17	18
19	20	21	22	23	24	25	26	27	28	29	30	31	32	33	34	35	36
37	38	39	40	41	42	43	44	45	46	47	48	49	50	51	52	53	54
55	56	57	58	59	60	61	62	63	64	65	66	67	68	69	70	71	72
73	74	75	76	77	78	79	80	81	82	83	84	85	86	87	88	89	90
91	92	93	94	95	96	97	98	99	100	101	102	103	104	105	106	107	108
109	110	111	112	113	114	115	116	117	118	119	120	121	122	123	124	125	126
127	128	129	130	131	132	133	134	135	136	137	138	139	140	141	142	143	144
145	146	147	148	149	150	151	152	153	154	155	156	157	158	159	160	161	162
163	164	165	166	167	168	169	170	171	172	173	174	175	176	177	178	179	180
181	182	183	184	185	186	187	188	189	190	191	192	193	194	195	196	197	198
199	200	201	202	203	204	205	206	207	208	209	210	211	212	213	214	215	216
217	218	219	220	221	222	223	224	225	226	227	228	229	230	231	232	233	234
235	236	237	238	239	240	241	242	243	244	245	246	247	248	249	250	251	252
253	254	255	256	257	258	259	260	261	262	263	264	265	266	267	268	269	270
271	272	273	274	275	276	277	278	279	280	281	282	283	284	285	286	287	288
289	290	291	292	293	294	295	296	297	298	299	300	301	302	303	304	305	306
307	308	309	310	311	312	313	314	315	316	317	318	319	320	321	322	323	324

With 36 days in a year, this is a 9-year calendar for the collective fairy groups that have gathered here on Earth. A year consists of 3 weeks. There are 12 days in a week.

Figure 9

Closing of Book I

It is with deepest gratitude that I acknowledge the vast contribution that the folk from the fairy realms make in all aspects of nature. Their roles on Earth and in the cosmos have become far vaster, standing toe-to-toe with the roles of the angels. This is a gift of acknowledgement to them by the Mother of All Creation for the great service they rendered in safeguarding the sacred knowledge within the jewels during the time of illusion gone-by.

All of the groups of fairies that have returned to Earth from the planetary systems mentioned in this book, originally came from Earth (the Earth-Fairies from Lyra being the only ones who kept their identity). Their triumphant return heralds a most significant event: the imminent removal of the veils between the realms. This signifies the dawn of humanity's adulthood, as we take our place among magical beings within the cosmos.

My day-to-day routine has been filled with miracles since the beginning of 2005. But I have had to take great precaution to keep even the masters in my classes from seeing many of them. The photographing of the two god-children in October (which I am unfortunately not able to publish, but have shown to my students) seemed to have been a breakthrough; and photographs of what would be regarded as "super-normal" seem now to be permissible. It has been heart-warming to see with what openness long-guarded secrets are shared by these kingdoms with man.

The purification that has taken place during the Earth's ascension[28], although still unseen by the masses, is discernible to them.

As this magical week comes to a close, both the Arcturian Fairies and the Unicorns are waiting to have us produce books about their

28 See *Secrets of the Hidden Realms* for details on the Earth's ascension process, and *The Ring of Truth* for the massive cosmic changes that have taken place.

magic. The Unicorns have given the title of their book: "The Gift of The Unicorn: Sacred Secrets of Unicorn Magic (A Journey into the Deep Laws of White Magic)". Again, the book has to be written in one week only. Other groups, which cannot be named, are also waiting to share their information. It is therefore with great excitement that we enter a future in which information flows freely, and can no longer be obstructed.

I honor the readers of these books who, through the purity of their hearts, are pulling forth the information. You are indeed the bringers of a new day, refusing to live within the prison bars of the five senses. The more profoundly you allow this treasured information to affect your lives, and the more respectfully you treat it, the more miracles that shall be allowed to be revealed.

My life is dedicated to you who are the light-workers of the Earth, and to the interconnectedness of all life.

Book II

The Mystical Kingdoms

(see: www.interdimensionalphotos.com)

Photo of a Fairy taken by Carol Comerford in Battersea, Ontario
Figure 10

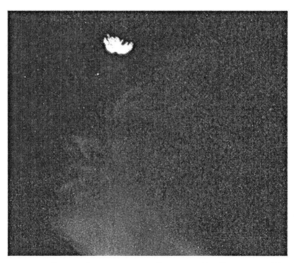

A green fairy hovers in front of Almine's face
Figure 11

The Mystical Kingdoms

Introduction

For the game of individuation to take place, the illusion of space has been maintained by a trilogy of three cardinal reference points: the cosmic space has been maintained by man, the Mystical Kingdoms and the Star Races.

In man's ascension that has taken place in earnest since 2005[29], he has changed from a very dense being to one that is far more ethereal. This is difficult to ascertain since we have no point of reference – everything we encounter has changed likewise.

When something transfigures to a less dense state, latent resources are released, such as power, life force, etc. Because like the ocean, the state of one area having more density than another is not tolerated within cosmic life, the released resources go to the least dense place. In this way as we have become more ethereal the star races and hidden realms have become more physical.

The two-dimensional 'television' screen created by these three components for individuation must now close. The linear method

29 Suggested reading: Secrets of the Hidden Realms

of creation that has produced weaker and weaker generations of individuations, as well as linear change, is coming to a close.

The way to form life in Oneness and not through illusion is an alchemical equation. By bringing certain components together, the leveraging of life into a higher form takes place. Long have tools, secrets to help man understand, and powerful ceremonies of awakening been safeguarded to be brought forth at this time as gifts of grace to humanity; a momentous occasion as channels of communication again open between man and the Mystical Kingdoms.

The Angelic Kingdom

THE ANGEL SCROLLS

Found in a Hidden Library in Iceland

1. Aresprethavi   Harmony   (Golden Light)

2. Mishelastruminach   Absolute Peace   (Lavender)

3. Vrupretravelavi   Surrendered Presence   (Rose)

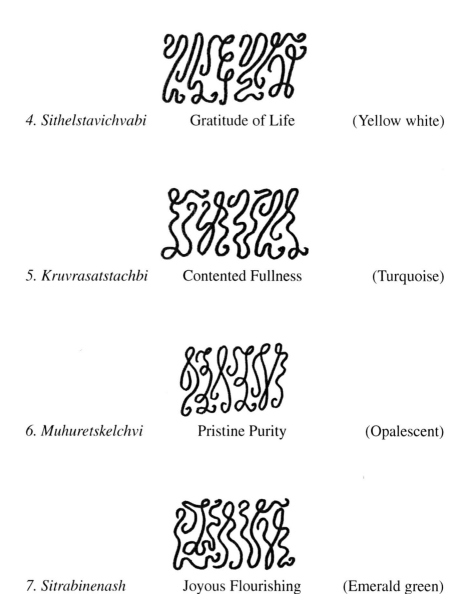

4. Sithelstavichvabi   Gratitude of Life   (Yellow white)

5. Kruvrasatstachbi   Contented Fullness   (Turquoise)

6. Muhuretskelchvi   Pristine Purity   (Opalescent)

7. Sitrabinenash   Joyous Flourishing   (Emerald green)

Translation of Angel Scrolls

WRITING FROM ICELANDIC LIBRARY

Received by Eva

TRANSLATION OF THE ANGEL SCROLLS

Before, in the Dream, to the order of the Rose and the Cross[30]
Angels brought knowledge once given, now lost
Of the powers of alchemy and the letters of humanity
In two octaves of notes that make twenty-six

Descending and ascending from the note of G
Two octaves of notes and letters of twenty-six
Each has a value, embodied by a race from the stars
Complemented by Earth, like a symphony from afar

The Earth as the pivot point has a central sun
It has two values while other planetary systems have one
The number thirteen is its masculine
Twenty-six is its feminine

Add them together into androgyny
And life is leveraged through Alchemy
Into that which is changeless yet ever newly-birthed,
To restore man's harmony and for a leap in consciousness on Earth

---

30   The Codes of Power given to the Rosecrucians by the angels during the Middle Ages.

The Key of Power of the Rosecrucians

Rosecrucian Square

For years Almine has been receiving deeply mystical information on different forms of Alchemy. Some of it, like these symbols depicted here, have been in the code of the Rosecrucians.

ROSECRUCIAN EQUATION

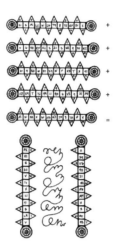

The letters and numbers have until now not been properly understood as to their origin and values. The angels, who gave the Rosecrucians their alchemy, give the key to these mystical symbols and the power behind them.

KEY OF POWER OF THE ROSECRUCIANS
THE QUALITIES OF THE LETTERS

A.	Antares	Becoming a wellspring of abundant life
B.	Ursa Major	Endless delivery of joyful surprises
C.	Orion Kaarit-arach	Absolute authenticity
D.	Orion Amphapabian	Power through depth of expression
E.	Arcturus	Surrendered trust in life's unfoldment
F.	Alpha Centauri	Expression of Oneness as relationship
G.	Andromeda Barugala	Graceful transition to fuller expression
H.	Andromeda Kaarsana	Refined awareness of Self as All
I.	Sirius C	Exquisite enjoyment of the adventure
J.	Lyra	Mindless omniscience
K.	Pleiades	Spaceless omnipotence
L.	Venus Melaganiga	Timeless existence of Oneness
M.	Klanivik Masculine aspect	Unstructured forming of beauty

THE UNSEEN PLANETS

N.   Huspave   Acknowledgement of life's unknown blessings

O.   Kruganet   Profound simplicity

P.   Uvelesbi   Beginningless life

Q.   Kaanigvit   The illumination beyond light

R.   Hubelas   Soundless symphony of life

S.   Piritnet   The newness of eternal changelessness

T.   Vaa-usta   Masterful expression of unfolding Oneness

U.   Graanuchva   Newly unfolding changelessness

V.   Bru-aret   The wonderment of timelessness

W.   Selbelechvi   Recognizing oneself in all things

X.   Husvaa   Communication beyond the senses

Y.   Minut   Beyond emotion into exquisite feeling

Z.   Klanivik
Feminine aspect   The contented passion of existence

PHOTO OF A DRAGON TAKEN BY
ANDREW GILHAM ABOVE GLASTONBURY TOR

Figure 12

PHOTO OF AN ANGEL TAKEN BY RAJ NARINDER

Figure 13

THE ROSECRUCIAN NUMBERS
OF THE KINGDOMS

1. The God-kingdom   Clarity through
                                    stillness

2. The Lords of Light   Poise through
                                    relinquishing
                                    perspective

3. The Dragons   Playfulness through
                                    enjoyment of life

4. The Giants   Creative expression
                                    of divinity

5. The Angels   Purity through
                                    mindlessness

6. The Griffins   Reverence through
                                    appreciation

7. The Mer People   Endless wonders
                                    through awareness

8. The Twitches   Creating spontaneous
                                    truth

9. The Magical Horse Races   Enjoyment of self as
                                    the One Life

10. The Devic Kingdom   Fluidity through
                                    lightness of being

11. The Fairy Kingdom
Claiming all resources as the One

12. The Kachina Tribes
Infinite life of joyous exploration

13. Humanity
Embodying the Oneness of All

14. The Mystical Large Serpents
Embracing boundarylessness

15. The Mystical Bird Tribes
Claiming the magic of life

16. The Tree People Bekbavarabishpi
Claiming the fullness of all resources

17. The Elfin Kingdom
Increased experience through gratitude

18. The Embryo Beings Glaneshveeva
Sustenance through the Self as the One

19. The Cat Races
Being One with life's spontaneity

20. The Pixies, Gnomes Dwarfs
Embracing our vastness

21. The Fauns
Unwavering surrender

22. The Archetypal Spirits of nature
Unclouded clarity of timeless existence

23. The Wise Ones[31]	Freedom from self-reflection
24. Actuungi The humanoid bird tribe also called the Kurutaka	Unchanging innovation
25. The Braaminhut[32]	Ecstatic union
26. The Human Gods	Expression of divine perfection

THE SIGIL FROM THE KAATCHRUKI
FOR CREATIONLESS CREATION

Received by Shelley

---

31 See *Secrets of the Hidden Realms.*
32 See *Opening the Doors of Heaven.*

A SIGIL FROM THE WISE ONES –
THE CONTRADICTION OF KNOWING
THE UNKNOWABLE

THE ALTERNATING EMPHASES OF THE EXPRESSION OF THE ONE LIFE

THE SIGIL FROM THE ACTUUNGI, THE HUMANOID BIRD TRIBES

(also called the Kurutaka)

Arasang Biliva Nanvush Hayava

MESSENGER ARCHANGELS OF
THE HIDDEN KINGDOMS

1. The God-kingdoms — *Kaalava-vreblik*
2. The Lords of Light — *Usutaa-praaruk*
3. The Dragons — *Nusuta-pilek*
4. The Giants — *Hersavaa-aklet*
5. The Angels — *Kiharus-arstaa*
6. The Griffins — *Viset-aklut*
7. The Mer People — *Eles-miret*
8. The Twitches — *Kaarat-viblut*
9. The Magical Horse Races — *Arak-helsta*
10. The Devic Kingdom — *Visper-aruk*
11. The Fairy Kingdom — *Elestrak-berut*
12. The Kachina Tribes — *Kasa-ukusuvru*
13. Humanity — *Baarsut-ekelvi*
14. The Serpents — *Erskavaa-nunit*
15. The Bird Tribes — *Arsha-bravahut*
16. The Tree People   Bekbavarabishpi — *Urskante-ruravach*
17. The Elfin Kingdom — *Baarnava-savavi*
18. The Embryo Beings   Glaneshveeva — *Arch-anat-skuvaa*
19. The Cat Races — *Elbisharek-struhava*

20. The Pixies, Dwarfs, etc. — *Trehanunabach*
21. The Fauns — *Ersklave-Tristunet*
22. The Archetypal Spirits — *Plihu-varanet*
23. The Wise Ones — *Ratvi-utrene*
24. The Actuungi — *Usva-kliher-rutv*
25. The Braaminhut — *Karasarva-i-u-ane*
26. The Human Gods — *Kaalanesh-ustet*

The Griffins Speak

The Griffins Speak

At times the eons and the times that we have spent
Seem never-ending as though something their conclusion prevents
The Infinite's embodiment could not see
That Creation could not perfect be

Based on duality, the cosmos could only attain
That which could be achieved within the illusional game
Furthermore, the Infinite continually would
Strive for Its Being to be understood

That which is real a contradiction remains
For never does the Infinite remain the same
Ever newly expressing though unchanging it stays
To the finite understanding it incomprehensible remains

The addiction to doingness the masculine emphasizes
As though beingness is not as valuable in our lives
This prevents the healing of duality's ways
Prolonging that which causes us in cyclical change to stay

Nanekchuk balack Bruharat

No error anywhere can be found

Transmission from the Mer People

TRANSLATION OF THE TRANSMISSION
FROM THE MER PEOPLE

How did it happen that the shadow gods were able to create alternate realities that lay like a fish net over the treasured perfection of the cosmos? To tell this, we tell also of the origin of war. The masculine elements of the cosmos, acting independently and without regard to its feminine, lost the greater inclusive vision. The cosmos went into egocentricity. The directions of an illusional inside and outside developed. The masculine became addicted to testing its skill against opposition. The addiction to conflict began, as did the inner war between the genders. The masculine gave more and more power away to increase the conflict by allowing more and more alternate overlays of distorted realities to form. The feminine within suffered as the masculine chose the illusional of an 'external' feminine, ignoring and reducing the quality of life.

Come to the place where the Mer clans meet[33]
Let the addiction to conflict forever cease
Let the embodiment of the One enter into androgyny
That the suppression of the feminine may no longer be

Six Mer Clan Leaders	Clan
1. Vrooniminaneem	Waaroom
2. Waahuunee	Oonim
3. Velooom	Vavoom
4. Wehaanoom	Vuveem
5. Kaanooneem	Mehanuneem
6. Baaheeneem	Sashee

33 Curacao.

THE ORIGIN OF GUILT

The Infinite's masculine knew it was just a game
But not knowing this, Creation in earnest the game did play
"Let us help all creatures, freedom to gain"
Thus to assist, a contract was made

The Infinite's masculine wanted them to enjoy the game as well
Thus came the origin of guilt of which we tell
Not able to maintain the pace of the game
Creation itself for the failure did blame

They feared, as the stakes got higher and higher,
That more from them would be required
They hid from the Infinite, cutting themselves off from Source
Aging and death were born as they were severed from resource

Not understanding that this was their own doing
They thought it to be punishment that death was ensuing
Then even more did they feel the shame
For the repetition of cycles they themselves did blame

Nirichta selvavi mishet astu serve-va

Through integrated Oneness healing comes

The Clans of the Fauns

Pursetaa-barskparknut

THE CLANS OF THE FAUNS SYMBOL

Sukarat nichte palish asakenit

The balance of life rests within the individual

Kirik asat blublahek sekeve nisarat

Too long has life been defined by what is not

Kakalesh mishat nenete asarak harahus

Find that which supersedes all expectations within

BEYOND MEDIOCRITY

Writings from the Fauns

"You need me to create excellence, the masculine whispers
convincingly.
Do not dwindle into inactive peace's sad satiety."

The masculine has guidelines and standards of excellence and fun
Like a thief it robs the authenticity of everyone
It is addicted to stress in order to feel alive
But within the inactivity of peace, no one thrives

To live means to engage in the game
Then life is unreal and death the same
Disengage from the labyrinth designed by mind
That is not life; there's yourself to find

FINDING YOUR ETERNAL SELF

Seek out the games of distress you've designed
Eliminate the labyrinth of complexity created by mind
Uproot too your desire for peace
Happiness does not lie in a life of ease

Neither ease nor distress within
Oneness exist Intense rapture and the sweetness of bliss
Cannot begin to describe what in Oneness abides
When Realness reveals itself as we shed the illusions of life

Nachsur avek kluklaknet asar blahuk

Find the greater life by letting the lesser go

Messages from the Fairy Clans

The Queens of the Fairy Clans

1. Siti-vilivi of the Glen Fairies

2. Winiyona of the Forest Fairies

3. Nananiya of the Mountain Sylphs

4. Kikipa-pihi of the River Slyphs

5. Sihiniwayeni of the Lakes and Lake Lands

6. Priti-binistri of the Ocean Fays

7. Silvibluhini of the Middle Earth

FROM THE FAIRIES

Disengaging from the Game

Let the game be pleasant, no more conflict and strife
No more to believe the illusory game to be life
The harmony within, of not believing ourselves to be confined
By the imagined boundaries of the Dream we left behind

Through the heart of a flower or the eyes of a child
See through the appearances to the real behind
Where a magical world illuminated from within
Awaits recognition for it as a reality to begin

Mini maka piti veriveti nanu asiviti huspi nasarut kiviva

When you wipe the fog from your eyes, you will see the real

EQUATIONS TO REMOVE THE ILLUSION
FROM ALL BEING'S VISION

1. Eliminating the illusion of lack +
   Eliminating the illusion of abundance =
   Access to all resources for joyous manifestation

2. Eliminating the senses as obsolete tools +
   Knowing all within our Being as the One =
   Knowing all as oneself

3. Dissolving the game of conflict with shadows +
   Eliminating all addictions by coming home to Oneness =
   Androgyny as the giver of harmonious dynamic balance

4. Contented exploration of beingness +
   Delightful uncovering of what is =
   Surrendering to the contradiction of existence

5. Accessibility to all resources through boundlessness +
    Eliminating all standards of mediocrity =
    Unspeakable excellence through living in Oneness

6. Fearless freedom from all memories +
    Eliminating all egocentricity or expansion =
    Stepping off the treadmill into higher life

7. Becoming One with all +
    Eliminating the illusion of the need for power =
    Immediate revealing of perfection

8. Living from freedom of boundaries +
    Eliminating the illusion that there is any need for change =
    At Oneness with the unfolding perfection

The Kachinas – Tribes of Innocence

Transmission from the Kachinas
The Flower Beings

Among the Kachinas before life fell
A tribe of beings among us did dwell
They left for Sirius and Arcturus too
When consciousness slept and darkness grew

In stones their fossilized remains are found
Restore them to Earth that their gifts may abound
Purity can be stained, it is therefore illusory
The true Being of the Infinite has incorruptibility

These Kachinas represent this quality
Among man let them and this quality again be seen

FOSSILIZED REMAINS OF THE LOST KACHINA TRIBE THAT REPRESENTS UNTAINTABLE AND UNSTAINABLE INCORRUPTIBILITY

Photo by Karen Folgarelli
Figure 14

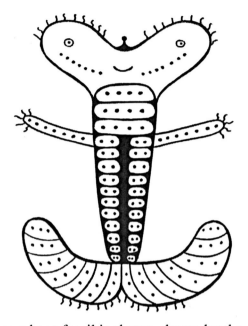

The Kachina whose fossil is shown, drawn by the oracle Eva

Elves, Pixies and Dwarfs

THE ELFIN KINGS

1. Petlbufpastra

2. Bamelheflbut

3. Ufelbramanit

4. Krugelnatbrafbablut

5. Satlbufpata

6. Hitnabrubasba

PIXIES

THE SATLBIHINI AND THE SATLBI

The ascension was frantic, yes it was so
But with dwindling resources war was the only alternative we
know
Thus a few did labor that others may sleep
Safe in their beds in an environment of peace

The Earth is not poisoned, by bombs stripped bare
The masculine knew this and did his share
Malign him not, increasing the opposition was done for a cause
He provided cosmic sustenance by making this choice

Kiti savi pirhit nesi na usu tihina mitisuane

Let nature thrive as the gates to resources open

DWARFS

The heat of the Earth has increased
As the suppressed feminine fumed and seethed
Klanivik has been at war with itself
The heat this produced within the Earth swelled

Let Klanivik open, now it's at peace
That the pressure within it may gently release
Like the oyster the pearl, a treasure it keeps
The cosmic life force center within it sleeps

Let this gem shine forth that the Earth may become
To the eyes of all, the glowing central sun

The Dwarfs of Danagaan

The Cat People

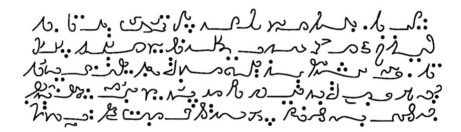

Zhong zetviva a auf bet klugat zelaver
Ut ra vat kleg nu nes pele gabaa uvaa
Staa belevee. Gabaa us vle u sa u naveesh
Kulu esh vraa vee zhaa una bleesh nanuvee
Vri vaa uleesh mi straa uzhing klavaa nut.
Zhong-galabruk spe utlaa kli u neesh

Cat magic was kept from the very beginning,
When land on Earth was all in one place.
We were the frequency keepers.
We mapped out the frequency bands and kept them pure.
We were hidden by the One in a dimensional pocket.
She promised to come for us, the Zhong-galabruk.

Nuchtraa beesh pelavee berznu stau gleek vershbaa.
Pru uvanee ske u eleveesh avrim uglechsti uvelebeesh bizet vi-esh
nu em

There are but a few hundred of us left.
The wait has been long. But all have been faithful to the Mother of
beautiful light.

Vileesh Zhong-galabruk pleusvamaa beleveez unet klavaa.
Sku bel taa uznasaa beleveez uklaa uznet belenu staa u belevee krunaa.
Gel zhon gnaa spaavi. Kernaa spuu assvaa.
Te ele nus pele huzaar kel una vi-eesh staa vaa.

OPENING THE GATES OF ABUNDANCE

Through eons of being cut off from the never-ending supply from Source, the cosmos has run low on resources just as embryonic fluids for a fetus can only sustain it for so long. The last time this was the case the Great Depression occurred. The bubonic plague that ravaged Europe was another such time. Disturbance in weather and climate is another indication that cosmic resources are low.

War generates energy through over-polarization, even though it is negative energy like the adrenalin rush a smoker gets. Many have waited for a positive solution to this dilemma; one that could tap into the Source of limitless supply. The Elves have safeguarded this secret and are now permitted to share it.

Within us is a portal consisting of 144 components – concepts of limitless supply that, when understood, unlock these components. Jointly they open a portal that permits us to become a conduit for the limitless bounty from Source.

We become as life force centers for the cosmos, replenishing its supply. The Law of Compensation (which applies in a confined 'space' such as the cosmos) decrees that we reap rewards for this service. It repays us with physical abundance and instant manifestation.

TRANSMISSION FROM THE
SMALLER CAT PEOPLE

Shadow gods arise when within the gods of light
Unused potential slumbers, casting a shadow by blocking light
When the gates of abundant life open within
The elimination of perpetrators will begin

No more shadows, no more opposition
We no longer need to generate energy through polarization
Behind the life force center a sacred portal lies
Called the Haaraknit, it opens to the One Life

Let it open in the masters of the Earth
That a time of abundant supply be birthed

THE ROOT OF LONELINESS,
ABANDONMENT AND DISLOYALTY

The cosmic masculine also has a feminine pole
In his over-activity their relationship was un-whole
Abandoned was she, always seeing that his needs were met
Not feeling lovable, she settled for feeling needed instead

Independence and co-dependence from the masculine's two poles
As vast cosmic bands[34] of comparison arose
The cosmic feminine totally dependent on the masculine became
As he for all determined the game

---

34 See *Journey to the Heart of God*

THE OVERLAYS OF LIFE

Like a garment they are; a hand in a glove
Composed of sub-quantum particles of light and love
The particles though unreal allow form's illusion
That we may play relationship's game without confusion

Illusional they are but they serve the play
For as long as we know it is just a game
Formed by a triad of lack we perceive
Created by blind spots that deliberately deceive

Only one more remained of power particles composed
The feminine's masculine interdependence sought
To bring peace to the cosmic family but all for naught
He created the Watchers to oversee compartments of life

Being hostile and false they secretly did undermine
The feminine seeking compassion the Watchers did embrace
They secretly schemed her to replace
For wherever self-abandonment does occur

The virus of cancer will certainly enter
A triad of needs and abandoned life
An overlay of reality creates, that truth does hide
Let the cosmic family within be healed

And truth no longer shall be concealed
If it disappears, no form will we know
Created by feelings of inadequacy
External validation and fear of responsibility

The Bekvabaravishpi - The Tree People

Transmission from the Bekvabaravishpi

Received by Karen

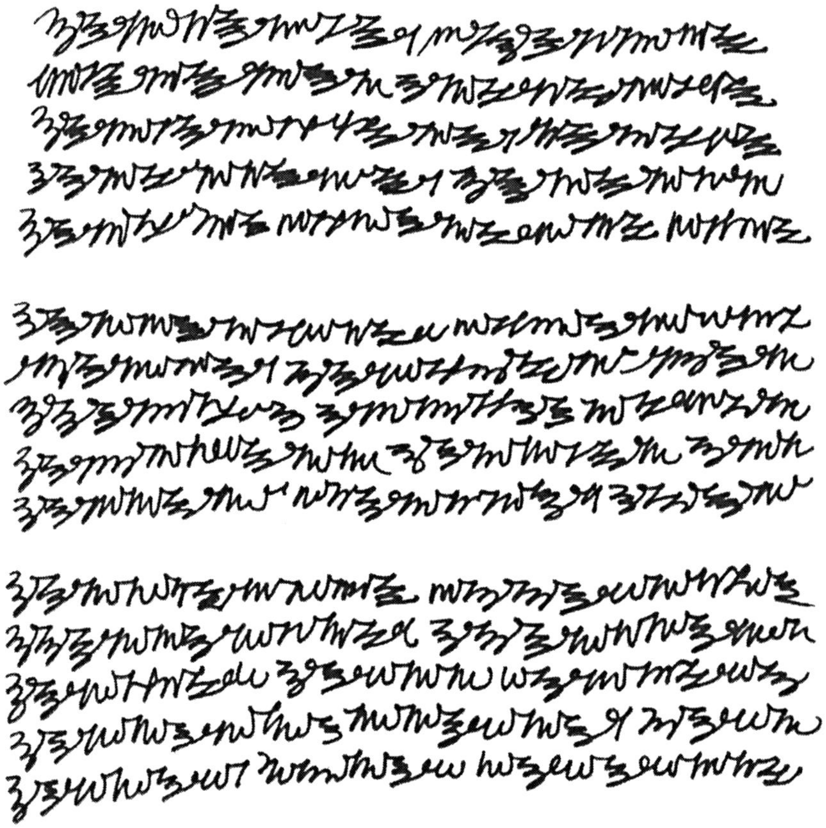

With opened hearts the masters shall sing
The Song of the One Life which new resources shall bring
Attraction, like that from a flower to bees
Shall radiate from these masters in order to keep

The creatures of the cosmos into old realities to retreat
Holding the cosmos like a little child's hand
Until all in self-sovereignty can stand All will be given the capacity
This great gift from the One Life to receive

No longer to wait for those who resist
When their overlaid reality is gone, they will cease to exist

There are seven overlays of reality forming individuated reality. Each is kept in place by three areas of perceptional flaws and self-abandonment. (For example: the 6th overlay has disloyalty, loneliness and abandonment, the 7th has inadequacy, the need for external affirmation and fear of responsibility.)

The masters of the planet have moved through to the 7th overlay, becoming sources of resources from the One Life to vitalize an ailing cosmos. The replenishing of the cosmos became necessary as the end product of cosmic life became much greater than anticipated, with greater refinement.

To keep the cosmos from recreating the old patterns and strengthening the old, obsolete overlays, the masters broadcast the specific songs that bring a feeling of fulfillment to the beings in the 6th and 7th realities, keeping them attracted to those realities like bees to a flower.

Although we all live as though together, beings are in seven different realities, living from seven different, alternate templates. Only the 6th and 7th are being held in place by the song coming through their hearts. However all realities are benefitting from the external resources that cannot be depleted, coming through the masters.

Those who resist this will eventually run out of the necessary resources to sustain them, since neither the life force center or the spaceless space behind it, will any longer be storing and producing the old quantum physics' particles (the building blocks of life).

They will by their own choice no longer be individuated but be absorbed back into the sea of Oneness.

The Large Serpents

The Oracle Shelley's and her Son Nate's Experience with the Large Serpents

A green and blue serpent came to speak to us this morning. Kanuikuk is his name.

"Instant pleasure over the hills
Relaxing the need, open to the mill
Preposterous lives need to be cleared
Honeyed, so sweet, magical release
Magnetic and wise we have become
But needed now a space to live from
Clear and soft, open and more aware
No judgment, just peace for all of us, so dear"

His eyes are red to paralyze his prey of fish and yellow when he is happy.

Nate drew a picture of him.

Drawing of Kanuikuk by Nate

The Principles of Abundance – from the Wisdom of Serpents

Understanding the Principles of Abundance From the Serpents

Introduction

Comprehension and perception have always been the means of silencing our fears; fears of non-survival, of a depression or lack.

Instead of succumbing to the fears of the masses and becoming subject to manipulation by those who stand to gain from economic chaos, let us stand in mastery. Awareness of the principles that form the foundation of an abundant and prosperous life will help us achieve this.

Let us not lend strength to dire predictions of economic collapse. We are the creators of our own destinies. A re- vamping of our lives away from the debt-ridden sham that our economy has become is inevitable. We can weather the storm and survive.

THE 144 PRINCIPLES OF ABUNDANCE

The Wisdom of the Big Serpents

1. Necheratsatve
Acknowledging of the source of all abundance as ourselves giving to ourselves increases the flow.

2. Mishinunask
The flow of abundance is an illusion. We have always had access to all abundance.

3. *Sivibaratparve*
Let our daily mantra be "I am abundance."

4. *Neskavabrut*
To consider the recipient's worth when giving is to close the sluices
of our supply, for to deny another's worth is to deny ourselves.

5. *Kiha-usavava*
To think of money as a base currency is to forget that all that exists
is the One Life.

6. *Blispa-ura*

The illusion of relationship is a game for the sake of delight.
Money is a man-made game within a game and should also be for
delight.

7. *Kirina-ubelespetve*

Abundance is living within your means with grace. It has nothing
to do with how much you have or earn.

8. *Nusarabi-eklavi*

The viewpoint that money must be earned reduces the possibility
that it can come from other sources.

9. *Usbakararu*

Treating ourselves with abundant care and nurturing is the first step to an abundant life.

10. *Utremishelvi*

The true currency of an abundant life is elegance combined with grace born of self-respect and is available to all.

11. *Archnat-husvavi*

Treat money with respect. It is the thread that weaves together the tapestry of human societies.

12. *Truhenemenemi*

Send a blessing with the money you spend, that it may bless the fisherman and statesman alike.

13. *Sihubelvi-uvre*

Money is the man-made lifeblood of society. It circulates, bringing back to you that which you send out with it.

14. *Kaarach-natvavesbi*

When we see our monetary resources as our security, we deny that our being is our sustenance.

15. *Sihuves-eklavi*

When money becomes the measuring stick of our achievements, our desire for wealth becomes an obsession.

16. *Nese-usalvavesbi*

To desire to live abundantly is as natural as the fish desiring the ocean. Money is only a small part of abundance.

17. *Iset-uhalesba*

Be lavish with yourself with those things that bring you joy. Awareness helps us find joy in simple pleasures.

18. *Achnaar-mishelvi*
To regret the loss of resources is to deny that we are the creators of
our lives and can create as much abundance again.

19. *Kurastaar-birat*
Some feel guilt at having too much and others at having too little.
Guilt clogs the arteries of supply.

20. *Utrenit-alsavi*
Some acquire to live, others live to acquire. In both instances
acquisition has become a need rather than a joy.

21. *Bitru-echnaru*
As the One Life, we are all things; there is nothing to become.
When we strive for more, we perpetuate impoverishment.

22. *Kurstebitburet*
Vigorously uproot belief systems that indoctrinate with perceived
status symbols and fabricated needs.

23. *Kalahachbavrit*
The weight of comparisons will impede us as we dance with the
abundance of life.

24. *Nisalhuraspe*

Comparisons will either make us feel poor because we have less or guilty because we think we have more. Each one has manifested their life in divine perfection. Let us honor this.

25. *Pihurskalvavi*

In seeing the poverty of another we are observing an impoverished part of ourselves. Fix within what is imperfect without.

26. *Ketrech-mishava*

When we bargain we bar ourselves from gain. The law of compensation decrees that life too will then short-change us.

27. *Ke-uhastar-esklavi*

Spend only what you have so that you do not become the slave of dysfunctional needs.

28. *Sutulehunas*

Budgets block the torrential flow of abundance. Plan, but hold lightly to your plans and expect abundant surprises.

29. *Verutbavelesvi*

As you wish for abundance, ask for the world if that is what you want. If your desire is not met, no matter – it was not a need but a preference.

30.*Karitmishba-el*

Stagnation of resources comes from ruts. Let the adventure of life
unfold anew in your life daily.

31. *Otrunatskalva*

If you desire flow to come to your life, do not hoard. Donate that
which you do not use and throw away clutter.

32. *Ruchtavipa-hunat*

See yourself as a steward of your possessions. Treat them with
respect and repair rather than replace them whenever practical.

33.*Kirasat-esalvi*
Those who take in greed deplete not only themselves but others as
well.

34. *Sutelniserat*
Taking resources for granted depletes them. All things dwindle in
the face of ingratitude.

35. *Kirabrutuhel*
When we approach anything with the question of "What is
the most I can get?" scarcity arises. Let us approach food with
appreciation rather than a need for nutrition.

36. *Nisabilevechvi*
When we listen to our inner rhythms our lives become fertile.
Barrenness arises when we do not listen to the song of our heart.

37. *Arstapla-uhat*
Loss of possessions is viewed by some as equivalent to loss of life.
It is often the catalyst to deeper living and vitality.

38. *Vrusekba-esetu*
A life of simplicity is not more enlightened than a life of
complexity. It just removes the temptation of having our
possessions possess us.

39. *Trinimire-u-anat*

Find the true pleasures of life. Man, having lost touch with what brings him joy, substitutes the veneer of purchased sophistication.

40. *Keserut-aresta*

Live life as a work of art. Let an attitude of graceful creativity enliven your financial affairs.

41. *Vrutrubarus-esta*

Paint life with a large brushstroke, but do not neglect the details. So too in financial affairs where small leakages can drain the reservoir of resources.

42. *Kaarch-urasbi*

In times of scarcity know it to be a temporary re- grouping that will reveal what really matters.

43.*Sihasklava*

When resources are scarce, let innovation blossom. This in itself can be a form of creativity shared with others.

44. *Erkba-usenetvi*

Adversity can teach us and our family more than many years of prosperity only if we enthusiastically pick up the gauntlet.

45. *Kira-sivelvru*

Life cannot take away without compensating us. A hole cannot be made in the ocean. Watch for new areas of abundance.

46. *Isel-iselka-uha*

It is through asking for what we want, while appreciating what we have, that we live the most powerful law of abundance.

47. *Nusbararut-uklave*

Each family member has a psychological poverty consciousness trigger. The housewife may need a supply of canned food to feel abundant. As far as possible, honor these triggers for your family.

48. *Kuritmistu-vibrat*

We are in a society that lures us into debt as a way of life. Resist this insanity as much as possible. Save first, then buy. Your greatest asset is freedom.

49. *Arathurspaklavit*

Not only is debt a form of enslavement, but it creates the unwholesome situation where we do not own the food we eat or the clothes we wear – the bank does.

50. *Arutprevitprahur*

How do we reduce a burden of debt? Get professional assistance and as in any long journey, do it one step at a time.

51. *Kununisarsta*

All addictions are the result of self-abandonment. The addiction of spending is no different. Balanced spending comes from balanced living.

52. *Virenimespahur*

The financial dynamics of a family unit indicate its flow of power. Where the assets and monetary control is lodged, there too is the power.

53. *Archarnot*

Money is crystallized power and the same laws apply. When it is hoarded, the universe conspires to take it away.

54. *Vilshpaver*

Life's fertility wanes when there's egocentricity. Spontaneous giving of the self creates an environment in which to flourish.

55. *Useta-minaruch*

When life becomes consumed with duty, the heart feels deprived. Life becomes impoverished. No money can compensate for that.

56. *Harasut-ekleva*

Envision carefully what you wish to manifest. Return to it several times a day, adding more detail. See it as though it already exists.

57. *Urchbarut-harestu*

Spend money as a proxy. As you give a dollar to a person in need, give it by proxy through intention to all who are in need.

58. *Nesaretvibarish*

In treating money as crystallized power, with intention empower what you spend money on. Taxes create amenities that better society - envision that.

59. *Usutu-hesklave*

The monetary system uses counterfeit value, pretending paper money has value. It must evolve to a barter system and beyond.

60. *Erklevibrasiva-el*
The ultimate goal of the evolution of the monetary system is that
we offer goods or services for what they are intrinsically worth to
us in trade – a voluntary trade system.

61. *Arknipribasuvael*
The evolution into a barter and voluntary trade system must begin
with us – even if it is just one step at a time.

62. *Esete-mishavi*
The communities of the future will function from a trust system
where all put their products and services to use and take what they
need.

63. *Nisitrananuspavel*

Frugality has nothing to do with how much we spend, but in how impeccably we refuse to squander energy through playing dysfunctional games with others and through resisting life.

64. *Uklevisa-usba-el*

When we labor with joy and excellence, drudgery to earn a living turns to a labor of love and creativity.

65. *Uhuvrasut-ekenechvi-vavru*

Send blessings with your work that the fruits of your labor may have increased value and leave the cosmos in your debt.

66. *Asabitvaret*
A production line can become a mantra when our attitude is one of
voluntary service to all life.

67. *Kuhele-ustrava*
Acknowledge with gratitude those who serve you and life will
support you.

68. *Kese-usalava*
In life's dealings, give the most you can and not the least.
Otherwise you leave yourself in life's debt.

69. *Husalnanetkleva*
Surround yourself with those who, like you, seek to give the most possible so that you are supported by winners.

70. *Ruchperpranavishper*
Shun those who seek the most they can get, that you may not be encumbered by parasitic vines.

71. *Nuselvevarabi*
There are those who seek to diminish your resources and achievements and those who try and profit from them. Neither believes they can achieve through their own efforts.

72. *Aktrahanesetu*

Enabling others to view you as their line of credit is to promote
disempowerment and a misplaced sense of entitlement.

73.*Ruchtrerig-ashva*

If you give to another, consider the extent of his need. He may
need a skill, or to be put in touch with an agency or a month's rent.
Next, consider your capacity to give.

74. *Oselena-skavir*

Give that you may get. He who generously assists where he can,
opens the sluices of cosmic supply.

75. *Utrekverbitvranu*

Where families have been supported by large debt structures, a necessary economic re-adjustment is to be expected. Substance must replace such hollowness.

76. *Kirsprahu*

To the caterpillar in the cocoon, his metamorphosis seems catastrophic. The financial system likewise must transfigure.

77. *Sitklevrenavu*

Do not lend empowerment through attention to financial doomsday predictions. Prepare for the worst and expect the best.

78. *Uskeleperenu*

Trust in the resilience and ingenuity of man and in one lending a helping hand to another to successfully navigate a global recession.

79. *Aktrabar-rutvavi*

Let recovery from financial setbacks become a family affair that children may learn how to cheerfully and optimistically adjust to life's vicissitudes.

80. *Petribarprevu*

Life presents daily doors for you to knock on. Be alert to these multiple opportunities. Some may open and some may not, but knock!

81. *Arekstavar-aresni*

Do not hang back from knocking on doors before you because you do not know whether you want to enter. Wonderful surprises may lie across that threshold.

82. *Husetminur-haresbi*

Instead of spending energy on casting blame, winners spend it in accomplishing. This creates the opportunity for life to even the score by recompensing you.

83. *Eklevibretsalvavu*

Failure is not lack of success, it is being afraid to try.

84. *Archpa-minurparvet*
To measure our success by possessions is to be enslaved by the
false values of social conditioning.

85.*Lispera-unesvi*
Self-pity creates a downward spiral in our circumstances, since
what we focus on increases.

86. *Rikpertresubar*
Self-importance stemming from past accomplishments and pride of
possessions blocks the manifestation of an even greater future.

+⊣K⌃H

87. *Iselvri-isevechvi*

Fluidity is the key factor of success in financially trying times.
Consider temporary options and multiple jobs.

YW⊣⌐⊣I:

88. *Niset-arusprehit*

Time management is essential when demands increase. Use a
structured and disciplined approach, leaving time for fun with
loved ones.

N⊿⊣⋔⊿:

89. *Kiranut-useltra*

The Earth groans under the weight of refuse from prepared food
containers. Returning to whole foods is not only economical, but a
return to conscious living.

90. *Viselvu-nisbaret*
Scientists have found we entrain the Earth and vice versa.
When we cultivate fertile gardens, the Earth restores our fertile
abundance.

91. *Kelhe-etrevibareru*
By cutting ourselves off from nature we lose sight of sound values
and become steeped in blind materialism.

92. *Nachpa-blavushvi*
Knowing the Earth to be our source of supply and our being to be
our sustenance, we have established the foundations for prosperity.

93. *Arusparva-kererut*

Think of money as love. Give freely where you can and it will
return freely.

94. *Haris-esklavu*

Would you bargain with your love, giving only as little as you can?
Then why would you bargain and withhold money?

95. *Suthit-arsevrunu*

To allow ourselves to pay the over-inflated prices masquerading as
sophisticated trendiness is to support self-important exploitation of
society.

96. *Viblik-aretvrenut*

By doing your work with a glad heart, as a service to life, you become a cause rather than an effect.

97. *Sutvaa-arsekla*

All successful achievers know that they write the script of the play of their lives. As they see themselves as abundant, so they become.

98. *Etsilbihar-nursta*

In taking time for deep meaningful living, like watching the dawn, we know our joy. Joy is the guidance system for our choices.

99. *Karuchpaher-uset*

Living from the fully conscious life of wholesome values puts substance behind our endeavors. Soulless activity is hollow and cannot support abundance.

100. *Klivabrahutspanu*

Do not let your work dictate the pace of your life. Dedicate time slots in which you respond to its demands. In this way it does not become the master and you the slave.

101. *Esetepirahet*

Neither abundance nor poverty exists within the Ocean of Life. When we know this, we are free.

102. *Viripamichba-er*
To see poverty in another is to disacknowledge the cosmic
compensation for any seeming loss.

103. *Kassabi-unaset*
Greed is born from seeing resources as limited, which in turn
comes from living a life of boundaries.

104. *Vibri-unar-sklava*
It does not matter how many hours you work if there is creativity,
passion and excellence being expressed; work has changed from
duty to joyous life.

105. *Situmisanesparhu*
Create a home, not a house - a place in which reverence is given to
the divinity of those who dwell in it.

106. *Viblesaraskranit*
Homemaking should be regarded as a form of worship through
service.

107. *Usatblanich-serut*
Create in whatever measure you can, a work and living
environment that expresses reverence for life as sacred.

108. *Arska-ekletvibrat*

Tolerance and respect for others does not mean you should allow disrespect of the sacred space in which you live and work.

109. *Iseta-nachsparut*

There is no form of work more important than another when all is done as an offer of love upon the altar of life.

110. *Ukluvris-aranasut*

Many find bankruptcy unacceptable and immoral when huge amounts of money were spent to incur the debt in the first place.

111. *Eseteprahut-arsta*
To refuse to declare bankruptcy when extricating oneself from debt
through other means is impossible, is like the moth refusing to
leave the spider's web on 'moral grounds'.

112. *Vilinisperut-ukle*
When we learn our lessons, life does not repeat or prolong
hardship. Life is an adventure of insight, not a punitive taskmaster.

113. *Kaalanat-uset*
Karmic repercussions for debt cannot exist, since there is no time
and within the One Life debt is an illusion.

114. *Etre-minis-verspa*
Guilt over incurred debt blocks future flow. Any beneficial change
requires acceptance of the present.

115. *Kuhut-alerklesbi*
Man microcosmically represents the debt Creation has accrued
by using the resources of the Infinite's Embodiment after cosmic
supply became scarce.

116. *Archpa-isetnut*
Abundance requires not only directed flow through generosity, but
containment. Allowing waste and drainage amounts to trying to
contain abundance in a sieve.

117. *Hutre-viliset*
Those who flourish in hard financial times are those who find
creative solutions, rather than focusing on the problems.

118. *Eskle-minirus*
When financial systems fail us, looking for solutions within that
failed system seldom works. Think outside the box.

119. *Urutrakve-irespa*
Redefine abundance as having all you need and not needing all you
have. Most mistakenly regard extravagant excess as abundance.

120. *Uharanatve-vilevis*

Your possessions are your stewardship. Repair them rather than discarding, that the garbage heaps on Earth may dwindle.

121. *Usanandabi*

Help where you can, but do not feel guilt about having while others do not. Uniformity stifles a society's development.

122. *Ekselvrivar*

Whatever you manifested before, your being is as capable of doing the same or better again. Live with hope and without regrets.

123. *Aknaspraruspleha*
To create a new paradigm of living, simplify your life so that the
life-enhancing aspects may reveal themselves.

124. *Utunasvevrubahar*
The soul justifies its excesses and indulgences through self-pity.
Uproot self-pity ruthlessly – it obscures truth.

125. *Archnitvrevasusklar*
Self-pity looks outside itself to be rescued. Self-responsibility finds
a solution.

126. *Perenut-vrehasversklu*
Simplifying life, like cooking with staples rather than prepackaged food, requires more time but reduces waste and expenditure.

127. *Kelsat-plahuranes*
By reducing acquisition, appreciation is found for what we have. Always looking beyond the horizon leaves the surrounding landscape unappreciated.

128. *Vivarek-minestra*
Believe in the bounty of life and claim it as your own by living generously and avoiding hoarding.

129. *Usaba-vibelestu*
Do not use money as a substitute for giving of yourself. It creates an imbalance of lack for you and others.

130. *Asanahuspeva*
Principles of abundance are first learnt within the heart. When we give with joy, resources multiply.

131. *Kaarsabitekla*
When we allow others to take from us and pillage our lives, our time and our resources, we keep them from accomplishing on their own.

132. *Vrubelelchnu-avi*

Massive industries and institutions are built to feed on the achievements and misfortunes of others. Surround yourself with those who believe in their own accomplishments.

133. *Velspa-urektrana*

Allowing those who unsuccessfully manage their own lives to manage part of yours, is as foolish as the patient trying to treat the physician.

134. *Mishpaplihenut*

Judge not a slow pace as more praiseworthy than a fast one. In timelessness the concept of pace does not exist.

135. *Ukle-viberestrevanu*

Celebrate success but do not take it seriously. Neither success nor failure can be ours when there is only One Life expressing.

136. *Asanahu*

Success and abundance are the only constants in life. We either align ourselves with them through surrender and trust, or cut ourselves off from them through opposing life.

137. *Plevi-avi*

Contemplate with praise the abundance of the stars, the snowflakes, the field flowers. For what you focus on, you become.

138. *Haarechnesba-aleskla*
We dwell in an ocean of abundance. We are limited only by our
ability to recognize what is available.

139. Sitinatvi-perere
Abundance is a bottomless pit when it is defined as increase. We
live in elegant sufficiency when we gratefully recognize we have
all we need.

140. Iktranu-speklu-aha
Self-confidence assumes incorrectly that it must create what it
needs. Humility recognizes the self as a conduit for eternal flow.

141. Avanet-hilsba

Many feel guilt because they have more, while others feel guilt because they have less. There will always be alternating areas within beingness where certain resources are more emphasized. Equalization produces mediocrity.

142. *Usekparuspa-ekleva*

When certain resources are emphasized in an individual's life, others are de-emphasized.
Discover with gratitude where your wealth lies.

143. *Visarat-minechvires*

When we neglect the feminine[35] within ourselves, our receptivity to abundance becomes inactive and life becomes barren.

144. Kivaranut-preha

When you receive and hoard, you have become the tomb of abundance. When you receive and give, you are the womb of abundant flow.

---

35 See the Goddess Archetypes in *Journey to the Heart of God.*

THE ALCHEMICAL EQUATION FOR
OPENING THE GATES OF ABUNDANCE

Becoming Conduits for the Cosmic Supply of Resources

POWER SQUARE FOR BECOMING
THE GATES OF ABUNDANCE

Transmission from the Twitches
The Bee Ceremony

A tool we bring with our song that you sing
Twenty-six sigils to place in a ring
Angry bees that kill and sting
Flowers are dying. A solution we bring

The honey bees of Earth are being exterminated
By killer bees that from a black light cosmos infiltrated
Flower seeds too from there have come
Confusing the bees with their alien songs

When alien flowers beckon our bees
Their black light makes our bees weak
When black light bees our flowers seek
The species' demise you soon will see

Silence the song of alien flowers to bees
That black light flowers on Earth shall cease
Let alien bees that destroy and kill
Not be attracted to Earth's flowers though our bees are
still

Let our bees multiply and for our flowers yearn
That balance to bees and flowers once more returns
The cosmic masculine for the shadow feminine
fascination felt
Reflected in the bee kingdom its own felt neglect.

The Bee Ceremony

THE TWENTY-SIX SIGILS TO PLACE IN A RING

Method

Create a circle with the 26 Rectangles
Stand in the middle of the ring, calling the 12 Kings of
The Twitches' Clans by name and requesting that the
Twitches help balance the Bee Kingdoms

KINGS OF THE 12 CLANS OF TWITCHES

Sigils received by Barbara Rotzoll

1. Nachtu

2. Bilspa

3. Areska

4. Kalavrit

5. Sutvlavit

6. Nerastu

7. Arutpelsba

8. Klusetvi

9. Bilihars

10. Trebarur

11. Artanut

12. Suklatve

Rectangle No.1

Rectangle No.2

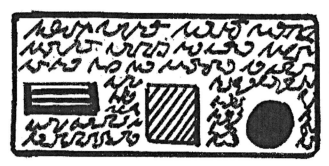

Rectangle No.3

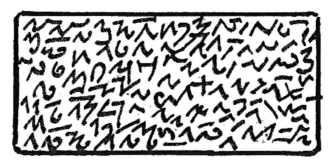

Rectangle No. 4

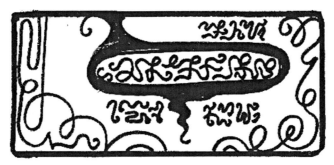

Rectangle No. 5

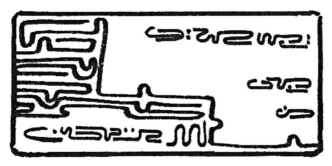

Rectangle No. 6

Rectangle No. 7

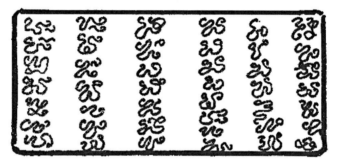

Rectangle No. 8

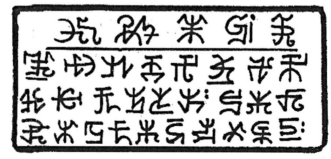

Rectangle No. 9

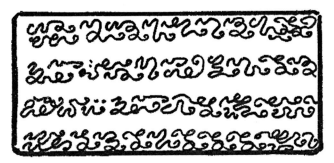

Rectangle No. 10

Rectangle No. 11

Rectangle No.12

Rectangle No.13

Rectangle No. 14

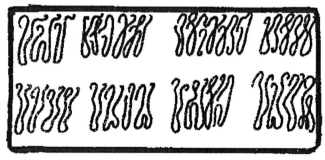

Rectangle No. 15

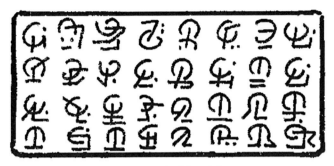

Rectangle No. 16

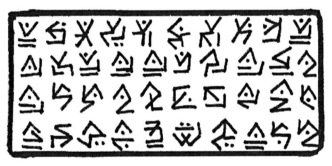

Rectangle No. 17

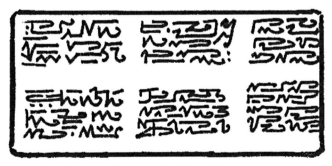

Rectangle No. 18

Rectangle No. 19

Rectangle No. 20

Rectangle No. 21

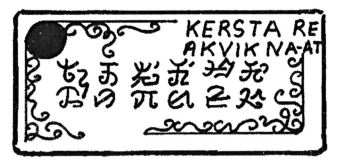

Rectangle No. 22

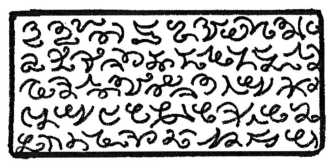

Rectangle No. 23

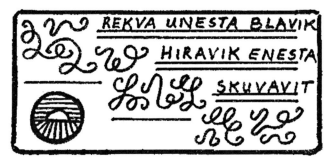

Rectangle No. 24

Rectangle No. 25

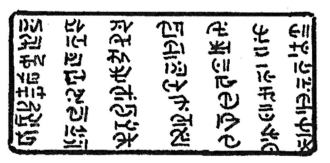

Rectangle No. 26

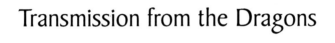

Transmission from the Dragons

THE RULERS OF THE DRAGON CLANS

1. Dragonit: The One of Regal Bearing
    purple, green

2. Sutanut: The One who Thunders Across the Sky
    turquoise, purple

3. Vrustabahit: The One with Golden Armor
    gold, red

4. Velebruspara: The Magnificent King
    violet, green, blue

5. Vlisparasuti: Dragon Queen of Radiance
   pale blue, lavender

6. Bergamorarut: Mighty Guardian of the Innocent
   red, purple

7. Peranuskelsarot: Dragon Queen of Luminosity
   white, gold

8. Vursklebasetvi: Dragon Queen of Multitudes
   yellow, orange, gold

9. Arasprahur: Golden God of Light
    purple, red

10. Nachpaspurar: Mighty Winged One
    black

11. Kelabar: God of Truth
    emerald green

12. Nachbar-rutva: God of Righteous Reign
    orange, gold

13. Nereti: Queen of Splendor
    gold, black

14. Kararahusta: Loyal Friend to the Infinite One
    violet, red

15. Gararuk: The Sacred God of the Holy Tongue
    black, yellow

16. Vruvasklarut: The Faithful
    yellow, white

17. Achnutherevi: Queen of Peaceful Reign
    pink, lavender

18. Sutabilepurera: King of Legions of Holy Ones
    gold, white, red

19. Nachtave: Goddess of Pristine Intentions
    white, opalescent

20. Veresatvi: Loyal Steward Queen of the Infinite
    gold, purple

21. Peretrubahar: Treasured One of the Infinite
    green, purple, blue

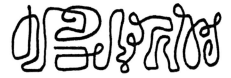

22. Nespakve: Regal Queen of Compassion
    white, purple

23. Virisetbalastar: God of Gentle Might
    red, white

24. Usata-balavu: Dragon King of Righteousness
    black, silver

Transmission from the Dragons

All have been given the resources of the One
To all seven realities has it come
Those who accepted it rose to a higher reality
Those who resisted shall no longer be

The masters to embody the missing frequencies
That caused the illusions of the three densest screens to be
Strongly expressed, they shatter the building blocks of life
Erasing the three densest overlays, clean they are wiped

No longer shall they pull the upper ones down
Now many shall rise, it will be found

Note: By dissolving the first (densest) reality, the tyranny of the
body is released.
The dissolving of the second releases the tyranny of gender and the
dissolving of the third releases the tyranny of mind.

Call hundred and forty-four angels of the sixth reality
To embody the qualities of untaintability
That the membrane may open between the seventh and sixth
More mastery will come by doing this.

REMOVING THE ILLUSIONS THAT HOLD OPEN OVERLAYS

1. Dissolving the suppression of emotion

2. Dissolving the devaluing of the feminine

3. Dissolving the search for sameness

4. Dissolving favoritism

5. Dissolving self-denial

6. Dissolving destructiveness

7. Dissolving the fetters of duty

8. Dissolving the need to control

9. Dissolving unauthenticity

SHATTERING THE ILLUSION OF THE BUILDING BLOCKS OF OVERLAYS ONE – THREE THROUGH FREQUENCY

1. Knowing the absolute safety of existence

2. Knowing only genderless androgeny

3. Being aware and appreciative of all life

4. Living in Oneness

5. Knowing self to be all

6. Enjoyment of unfoldment

7. Freedom through expanded perspectives

8. Acknowledging perfection

9. Authentic, deep meaningful living

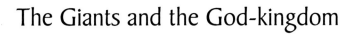

The Giants and the God-kingdom

The Giants and the God-kingdom
The Giant Gods

1. Gabruk – Giant with the Gentle Heart

2. Bruhat – Giant of Impeccability

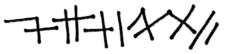

3. Hubaluk – Goddess of Compassionate Understanding

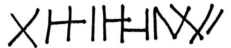

4. Manahug – Goddess of Nature

5. Bararasta – Giant of Sacred Government

6. Kuhubal – Giant of Sacred Guidance

7. Grunalag – Goddess of Fun and Celebration

8. Sablhut – Goddess of Sacred Ceremony

9. Arknat – Giant of the Environment

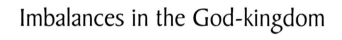

Imbalances in the God-kingdom

Transmission from the God-kingdom

The three lowest realities shall be wiped away
To the higher realities it shall seem like a single day
Realities four and five shall be purified
One hundred and forty-four angel gods shall be a task assigned

To open the membrane that between these realities lies
As they join, a new tone you'll find
The tone of self-renewal shall be when they are combined
Upgraded and healed and entirely purified

The sixth and seventh realities
Also through angels combined shall be
They embody specific frequencies
Self-purification and self-sustenance they bring

Now join together these vast realities
One shall be formed and there shall be no more sub-personalities[36]
Like a light in the dark the Earth shall shine
To all who can see light that's refined.

The Mer rejoice, the ocean's alive
The Hidden Kingdoms see the light that shines
No more depletion, no more scarcity
All are enlivened by the Earth's masters who conduits have been

The Angel God who Helps Balance Masculinity

Servalofprihinut

36 The inner warrior, nurturer, inner child, and inner sage as found in man.

THE NINE FACTORS OF BALANCING
THE MASCULINE

1.   Inclusive Masculinity
During the cosmic journey of mirrored matrices many
cosmic principles became reversed. Masculinity suffered
the same fate. Before individuated life formed, masculinity
as part of androgyny was not exclusive as it later became,
but inclusive. Because the feminine remained inclusive, the
masculine became incompatible

2.   Acting from Oneness
The desire for the masculine to dominate arose as a result
of the strictly masculine approach creating momentum in
cosmic ascension. The gestation period of the cosmos took
longer than expected and the resources were limited.

3.   Self-centeredness Changing to Integrated Oneness
No other poles of the Infinite's embodiment were capable of
supporting the masculine's hurried ascent to obtain another
energy source for the cosmos. This feeling of being alone in
his vigilance created self-centeredness.

4.   Acknowledging the Equality of the Feminine
The eons of not considering or consulting the feminine has
left a schism in which the masculine stopped listening to her.
No longer in communication, she withered in loneliness and
he began to undervalue her.

5.   Acknowledging the Feminine Part of the Masculine
Because the masculine had become a law unto himself, his
own feminine was suppressed and ignored. The benefit at
the time was that it sped up the pace before resources were
depleted.

6. **The Restoration of Hearing the Infinite's Voice**
Exclusiveness severs the connection with the One Life.
Alienation from hearing the highest choices occurs. The
resulting repetition of cycles serves to refine Creation
considerably.

7. **Surrendered Participation in Life**
The masculine's obsessive need to know was the result
of having to 'run up the mountain blindfolded'. Not able
to receive guidance from anywhere, he frantically started
mapping his way by dividing and labeling life.

8. **Reestablishing the Attraction to His Feminine and
Valuing Peace**
He invented shadows to wage war with in order to increase
the energy for the cosmos. He then became attracted to what
he had given away – the shadow feminine. When any part of
the self is given away, addiction forms. He became addicted
to the unreal and to war.

9. **Eliminating the Illusions of Inner and Outer Space**
The masculine's over-polarization caused contraction
to occur. He started looking for external answers. The
contraction caused a labyrinth of mirrors to form and the
confusion only aggravated his obsession to know.

Photos of Interdimensional Records

THE TABLETS OF THE HIDDEN REALMS

Almine has for many years translated tablets and records from inter-dimensional sources to reveal sacred information previously un-available to humanity. It is only in the last months of 2009 that some of her students have been able to obtain photographic evidence of the existence of these materials. See the following pages for examples of inter-dimensional photos of tablets previously translated by her.

Tablet translated by Almine months
before they were photographed.

Photographed by Barbara Rotzoll
Figures 15 & 16

Closing of Book II

Beyond the life of humanity,
Since the beginning of eternity,
In realms of mystery myriads dwell:
The Hidden Kingdoms of which we tell

Long-kept secrets at last released
A time when consciousness on Earth's increased
When man and faun stand side by side
To fold back darkness and stem the tide

Rejoice oh man, the time has come
The restoration of the Kingdoms have begun
Refined light once more shall be seen
By the eyes of humanity

Lift up your hearts, let them be glad
Joy is the gift we bring to man
Long have they toiled with no hope in sight
While in their midst dwelled the gods of light

(From the texts of the Scrolls of Infinity)
translated by Almine

Appendices

Appendix I: 100 Fairies from Venus

1. Taartxlklautsrkuvmn
2. Tlpimukvzsaalvkrrx
3. Plnkostvknaanjtrr
4. Prakaannstuklaapvrqs
5. Yakstuubliopevaas
6. Jaqtpuasraavlitkubatmog
7. Tsicklurksaakkrctvqs
8. Prqpnaallnzaurrinqxx
9. Uralaanaraqginaauipagaluo
10. Qlipaaxtafeukvaabi
11. Vildaaskpuurqlsnaailnmzq
12. Gatvztwaapkahvxlkaxx
13. Prxkolmitblukvrlaaxlapkq
14. Tkraalxqaknulwaainnxslaatvruq
15. Tapaarovmokaabinomandov
16. Tszlkraavilanqaapsloringusb
17. Taajkrsmuaathguinopdukwsmor
18. Kuaagqriaatnkhutfarrstkojg-
    weaakrmuaakoqstkobhtaarssd
19. Rmzzyatriikrrsaamudrraftuz
20. Laartopmirosuvtio
21. Igkrsuvtoaakaarusvtqmilsurto
22. Krasvtoquraakkity
23. Noopnarslupquvsrtyoknrsu-
    vynklortisma
24. Qrnstokuvnytrusknocrytasvuky
25. Klurakelpibraatulex
26. Vsrtxuakyaapasmorksyga-
    vospynksasraao
27. Plosnvorklaunyxostakiaao
28. Ullkarminaquranskillnaama
29. Grrslvosmmayklvusrgnkyslg
30. Knosrplqyvsokaan-
    rlexopneykngrsylklasasnpogm
31. Lsnopqtsuavraadosiatmrpqosaa-
    sytlrakjq
32. Krotsyjuvrkisrkauvaapqrz
33. Tvklipaacahaamnpqrullixk
34. Jansrakyuvsynarakoaapystrka-
    osraypo
35. Johmrkoptysmlysktrxu
36. Gsruptqsrviokaposygmarski
37. Gokrsyvarkaaspknyglsmroknig-
    sky
38. Vriqlamistnamistavaarupsky
39. Pushnaarvitlorensktrol
40. Svibolnutqurastaablukovaa
41. Qpzysmkrytoskyzrqogsatuv
42. Jqotsvrinquosraktyvnopslm-
    nrsjqyznd
43. Vsrkyqnostaacykrvosmxkycs-
    vunxovy
44. Osknyvlausrknymaskvrsuosh
45. Hosrkostyslmapoxyjnrstx-
    vakrsap
46. Ksoaprivqusnaporsnaazykso
47. Trasvanokpraticlynupsaa

48. Jlpqnrsyjkrabaskygonkryqsly-
    traskjfyz
49. Hrpqnrasmyakalayzajarkslmoc-
    gYuv
50. Qnsrtzyfmuaskrytazjanrsvquy
51. Zmroxnypgarokslyvxnrkozp
52. Glpzrkosltnyskrpojnyquvnoaxy
53. Glqysrvsrqanoslaqrasyzokosn-
    pzya
54. Kryslmaopgrqyzaasmnlpraky
55. Vsrqinapgonkrauosnsygkra
56. Qulranksaamertlinnkaasitarup
57. Laxrstonmakytsogrklsntnovsp
58. Noruskavaalomkestrapik
59. Nietsumakolvaarqusmitlimniva
60. Tuskaalinovaabistroqumaatev-
    skij
61. Ptilkamijoraaskilnatuquraa
62. Vilonakipuraalanissatopiqu
63. Omirskaalovnirkusnopirequtaa
64. Xtulaminsaavatorekamann
65. Jnqrsvaporsutavaaosrkiuvntys-
    aoaki
66. Tslkuvrnyasokrpsyvnulminrao-
    vaskyzlkg
67. Znokarpluvnistaarvokaaronuv-
    astayskjoln
68. Jsnoprkyjlostasakpojmlrkysm
69. Zsnopkaayravaotaikalagsnaaga-
    oksarav
70. Produvaradaanouplin
71. Glakausrkznayosnaganskrtay
72. Znasaraaxuokiytzrslpqrnosatuv
73. Vronskaataruktrakraskaali

74. Plakvaskaarutvatramui
75. Klutvasklutvremruvaak
76. Purekskiavaanobraalavnutilk
77. Gbryaaslurovnakuryla
78. Tuvirsklanokibolastoyicqura
79. Klarimasonetwaarutolmoyax-
    tomla
80. Umnarskqwlafiinaaraspotiks-
    voyamna
81. Vraminnatskowelaatanefrabi-
    latov
82. Tsintrovatknosvrushtalaawpuk
83. Zhivoranamilaquiraalablishi-
    naak
84. Ifdapraadmigkludedtyp
85. Kaatcbojnykolmnzbatom
86. Zqrzamaadbolkozytoarski
87. Zetvsikdfbvaajaavubinaaduh-
    vymz
88. Yrotoapzaavollagujaajrqlmp-
    toxrys
89. Krostyvwaacprakrstaaxyzuptlrk
90. Zuptxykalsraktprquvasyptxo
91. Prosaarkatyvsgokirypagsukry
92. Gsoprxstuviksrjopanqsytraz
93. Jlqospranijkusvtrsilaopkrl
94. Ubriocuraatlfaxpulbiu
95. Hufbaazupintasralop
96. Piudavlaatyomijhamnezbo
97. Ghirpaafelbaaswakvaasu
98. Pkiravestraakrugkraat
99. Zkivaraanipoulrvdaan
100. Vraatkruvtraaspaaku

Appendix II: 400 Fairies from the Pleiades

1. Suuleevaumbiishlaamishvaauum
2. Petelmiishpixeeemaaumbiiish.
3. Twirlabaalameriibaaaladuum
4. Viishlaaaevershmaalaavoom
5. Preevaaanaamasunamaalalaa-laaa
6. Veemaaaooshteuumehvaaadaa-naveh
7. Tuuleeevaaumpaapaduum-deedee
8. Veriiveeridaaoomgeeaaoom
9. Leedlhemmdaavaammuudaaa
10. Silvaanaanaekvaaoommaah
11. Baaariichnkorsiilaamtonaashi-ireema
12. Borshiimanoorkaaa
13. Simiishnariichvaasumneshbor-laaanakiimnaabushvishnasimka-larenomervsalish
14. Cantaleemavishna
15. Bolasaqvisaabiivaaaraanasiila-vushnishmaaraa
16. Kantishvaaasiiilaanaaamoyish-vanishkasaaa
17. Burnaalaaakaaasiimoona-pelaaasaavtiikotaa
18. Siiikoooraaalamiish-naakiishraasaaavasiitol
19. Biishkoolariishvapeeshka-ciiibaaaatasoupiraaalaaa
20. Aaalamaaaranakiishpataalaru-umsaaanaaa
21. Kaysoooraaasatiiivaniimsaaa-laanaaaap
22. Aaaashviishmaashooeeshmiich-shaaooeevaaoom
23. Mooshaaaooeevoshaarma
24. Oomasesheeaaosesheeaomesh-cheeaao
25. Mesheeaaaooeemauooeshee
26. Shemsehaaooaaeemeshem-ooaaee
27. Meshemwaaooeeaameshemooee
28. Shemsheeaamoesheeaaooesh-emshemaaooeshem
29. Ooaashemaaooeshemaaooesh-emaaooeshemaa
30. Vishaaemaaooeshemaashem-ooaaeshemaaesh
31. Maashemaashwaaeshem-aaooaashemwashemwaashem-aaa
32. Esheemwaaooshaameshem-waooshemaashemwemaashem-waa
33. Eeeshemwaaoooeshem-waaaooeshemwaaoooshemwa
34. Aaahnaaaseshwaaaoooshesh-emwaaaoooeshemwaaooshem-ooowa
35. Eeshemwaeeshmaawaaseeshem-waaoosheemaaaa
36. Ooshaashaawaashemaa-wooshaashemeshwaaaaoosh-emva
37. Ooshemwaasaameshaoooshaa-maashaasheshmaaoooeeemaaaa

38. Aameshwasesh-
    masheshoomaaooesh-
    maoooshesh
39. Aaamaaeshooaamaeshmaashaa-
    maseshmaaoshmaa
40. Ooomaasheemaaasheshmaaosh-
    maasheshmaaneshmashesh-
    maooaaa
41. Maasheshoooaaaooesh-
    maaesheshaaaoooaaooesh
42. Oomaeshaaseshmaaeshaamae-
    shaamaaeshmaaesh
43. Aamaaeshmaeshmaeshmaaesh-
    maanaaeshmaaesh
44. Eeemaaaoshmaaeshmaooshma-
    eeshmaaeshmaooesh
45. Maaeshwaamaaeshmaaoosh-
    waaeshmaoshmaoooshmaaa
46. Eshmaashemwaaaeshmaashe-
    vaaaoooeshmaoooaaa
47. Oooshemwaaaoooshooo-
    moaaaooa
48. Oooshemwaaaoooshiviiaas-
    haaavaaaoooaaa
49. Aaahaashaaoshemwaaoshem-
    waaaooshemwa
50. Oooaaashemvaaaooshem-
    oooaashemoooaaa
51. Ooaaashevaaavisherooomshevi-
    iooeshem
52. Oooaaasheeemwaaashaaaooo-
    shevaaashevaaaooshwaa
53. Aaaoomshaaaoooomwaaaviish-
    maaoooemwaaa
54. Oooshemwaaaoooshevwaaaooo-
    shevwaaaoooeshnaaa

55. Eeevshevwaashevwaaaoooosh-
    emwaaaooshemwaaaoooaaaoo-
    shev
56. Oooshemwaaaoooosheviiaashe-
    vaaoshamwaaoooosheviiaaa
57. Oooaaasheemwaaoooaaavesh-
    waaaoooaaashemvaaaoooaaas-
    hevtaaa
58. Aaasheeemaaashe-
    evaaaaaooooshvaaasheem-
    waaoooshaaa
59. Shevashaashemwaaaoshaamem-
    waaashaaaoooshaaviishesh-
    maaaakeshoshemveeewaaa
60. Aaavechmaakeshwaaaoo-
    shevkaweshwaaaooshevmavii-
    shmaaaooshaamaaveshmaaa
61. Oooaaaveshmaaaooshem-
    waaneshmaaaoooomakonesh-
    maaooshameoshmaaa
62. oooomaaaveeshmaaakeshmaaw-
    eeshmaaaooookeshmaviish-
    maaaoshkamasheeveshmaa
63. eeemeeeoshmaaaaoshem-
    waaweeshmaaoshemwaveeesh-
    maaoshemwavweeshwaaa
64. oooaaahmahsheem-
    kaaaooomaaaashem-
    kaaaooomaaaka-
    shevkaaaoomaashemkaavaaa
65. Oooomaaashemkaaooarashaas-
    hemkalaashaaiishnomeenshak-
    ereshnashaaaecklashemnaaa
66. Shemlaakeshmaalaafaashem-
    kaaoooshemlaakemlaashaaoosh-

313

emkemshaalaashaakemoshem-
raaa

67. Laashaanomaaashemoshemka-
lanaashemkaaoshemkemlaaa

68. Naaashaaakemlaaashemke-
moshemkemlaaanaaalaaaosh-
emkemlaaa

69. Jemkemlaasaashemkanaa-
laaaaoshemlaakemlashemkem

70. Aaamaakevshemkaaaooshem-
wiiaaaooshemkaweewaaaoo-
shevkaeeemaaa

71. Ooomeshkaveeewaaaoooaash-
kameshkaaaooanoveekaaano-
ashmekevshaaa

72. Ooomakaveeanaoomaka-
shevkaaaooomaakaavee-
shaaoooshamakeevaaa

73. Ooaashemkevshaaaooashemki-
ivaaooshemkaveenaaaoooaash-
emkevshaaa

74. Aaashevkaveshmaaakevshekma-
viimaaaviimanokevshaaaoshem-
wakevshaaa

75. Ashemwaviishaaaoshemwakem-
shaaaooshemkaveeaaaoshemka-
viiooaaa

76. Shemwakaviiaaaviaashemosh-
emkawavaawaoooshemviiem-
kaaaveshaaa

77. Emkaveshaamaaooshemkavi-
aaaviiemkaooshemooshemka-
viiaaa

78. Eeeshemeeoshemvaeeashem-
aawaaooshemkaveeaaaviiaaosh-
emwaaa

79. Ooshemwaeeshamwae-
shaamaooowaaaooshemka-
veemaaeshemkaveeaaa

80. Aaveshnaakeshemoshem-
waveenaaeshoshemkevmaaosh-
emkaveeenaa

81. Ooomakaveeshnaaeshke-
moshamnaaakeshammnovish-
naaaamkeshoshamnaa

82. Oooshamkeveeshnaaaveeshna-
komaashnaaveeshmaanokev-
shaakevchanoveeshaaa

83. Veeshanokevshaaakevsha-
noveeshnaaveeshnanokev-
naaaaaoshemkevnaaa

84. Keveshnaoshemkaveeshevnaa-
veeshnaaaoshemkaveenaavena-
koshemwaaa

85. Aaakevnoveenaakevshek-
noveenaaveenaaokevshakev-
shamoveenaa

86. Oooshanokevshaaooshavakesh-
naakeshoshamaaavaaaoshemva-
keevaa

87. Oshemkaveenaaaviinavokem-
shaaaoshemkaveenaaviinakosh-
emkaaa

88. Eeenaavokemshaaaoshem-
kaveemaaaveemaanokem-
shaaooshemkaviinaaa

89. Veenaoshemwaaaoshemnavee-
waaaviwaaoshemwaaaoshemka-
viinaaa

90. Viinavokemshaakemoshamvi-
iwaaaviiwaaoshaamwaaoshem-
kaviiwaaa

91. Ooonaavashemwaaaoshemka-
vemnaaaoshemkawenaaoshem-
waveenaaa
92. Aavanaveenaahveen-
amaoshaaaoshamnaveenaa-
maaoshemkoveeemaaa
93. Aaavaashemnoshemkalaafaas-
haanaamaaasaamshemkaalaa-
maa
94. Nemraakaalaakemoshamraajem-
kemraalaaoshemkemraa
95. Nooaaafaaraalaanaavish-
naakaanoraafaakeshlomenraa
96. Jemraakemraafemraakem-
raaoshemkemraafenraakemraaa
97. Oovaashmiishvaaeemaaviish-
pauum
98. Teetulviishmaaooemvaapliiesh-
vaaruum
99. Sentoorishiivaaatopishinaash
100. Aantoshiirilishkaapotaarana
101. Pantoraaalaatenkrishvaas-
hoonpaatiil
102. Tropaashnaavaatoooshisatishka
103. Kishpishtonishtaamaaaliikish
104. Peebuleemaaavaashbaaniish
105. Rommaadammaapeelaaaru-
umeshpliish
106. Kiiporishsuitiishlaaasoopish
107. Laaabishvatishnosaapaavaa-
keepotish
108. Aaaraleepuntishvaseepobish
109. Bliivaasvaaooshmiish-
baooeemaah
110. Eeevaaskaleemaaaeskaapleeum-
maa

111. Peleeushvaashpaaeespraave-
shuum
112. Meshkaataaniioohmashetlaati-
imashkaohmaatem
113. Ushkaapaachiidomashkaaaooaa-
maachidomvavaroom
114. Iinkaaveniishaaooeevenushkaa-
vavaaoolaaentaaiinkaooii
115. Meshkaaoaaemvestashkoom-
draashiinaashintashoomvatek
116. Doraataashkiilehmaaooiishchi-
idaameshaamtiiveneeeesh
117. Laaalkaaooiienkaaventiiindemi-
ishkaatemvaaachiin
118. Voshnaachekaalemkiishmonaas-
hchaaliishkaaliiimkaan
119. Belkraaesvaauumdaaaeshvani-
ish
120. Biishvauumpaaluumavechmaa-
dumbaael
121. Kuulishmaavelishvaashbaauu-
maa
122. Vaashmaumbaumbabadeluum-
vaeeh
123. Quetluushvaaoombaeevaauum
124. Miikelviishvaauumvaaeldauum
125. Briixlteeemaavoomaadaam
126. Freedlbaammuudaavuueem
127. Yentuuuveemaaslevaaber-
rvaauum
128. Strelaamishvaabeelaaum-
mvaamer
129. Peeeheevavoomaadeelaael
130. Reevaoomkeshvaplaviishdaoom
131. Beegellaavashdaoomdaveloom
132. Teelaakeerlavelmaaoombaaeh

133. Kliimaabellavaaumelaadauum
134. Pliimaduumvershdauumdara-amuueem
135. Eelmaavaviishmateluum-vaveechmaaeem
136. Kwirliishvaameesh-vaaeloomaaduum
137. Beevaashelaadaammuubaae-laadaam
138. Betelvashmaamaabuumaadaam
139. Preleprelevaamaaeshvaemma-dom
140. Baandicoatldeemaaveesh-baaraam
141. Chush-uusheemaavreemaaeldaam
142. Feyyelbaalaaeemsabellavechsaa
143. Pistillehvaaechsaaeemmaauum
144. Reelaalilalolaalekmaadee-laaoom
145. Vechmaapesheleemmaabi-ishmuuvaam
146. Aaaeshvaaasheemaaooshvakaa-reem
147. Preevaaviishbaamaaniishvaa-maash
148. Peerlaapeshbaavaaniishlaa-maaesh
149. Twertlvaaeeshoomaaveshpaeem
150. Viiraaaaoooolaaasaa-cheeeesoooroooaviii
151. Maanaaaaloooraaasisooonlaaa
152. Herroooeeeemishooonaaaroon
153. Aaaanoreeebiilalalooomli
154. Saaaanaaarimaaaayooshmoon
155. Liiilooorlaaabaaa

156. Biieemelellaeshvaaoomaaesh
157. Bremooeshvaakreemaaavaa-teeum
158. Miishvaaeshvaspaaiiuu-maavaash
159. Biishmaaniishpaaeshuuvaaniish
160. Braashmiirshvaaaraashlaarsh
161. Miiiirshoooomaavuuaashmi-ishba
162. Shuuaameephaaroooomiish-baaaaraaaam
163. Sheeeeviiaauumkeeliiaaruush
164. Sheenmiiaanuuaamulaaaaraam
165. Laashmiishaaviiraamaash
166. Maashaaraameeiiaauulvaaraa
167. Vaanaashuuaameeshaavaa
168. Biishbaashaamaareeliaam
169. Vendishlaashmeeriikaa
170. Laashmiiaanmeeoouum
171. Maaaaiiivaapaaaashaam
172. Meeiiaanaashiivaashiimeeshli-ibaa
173. Haaaashmeeiiooaavaaaash
174. Biishbaaaadraaaashveeoooosh
175. Maanaaaasheevaaoooomaaaalee
176. Graashmiivaashdoohooshmiish
177. Kristoloootoonaaateeeetopish
178. Mylooveebeeeatyuuurtoohish
179. Blakeeetolooorinaaapuishmaaa-leen
180. Helooomoooatooohlaaariish-kaaleet
181. Tripooolinishpaaatishnaapit
182. Braaastoloooonaaatlamiinaa-prishkateeetmish
183. Stolanoushaaatolooupaatish

184. Krasnovaaatolooonapishka
185. Brostaaalitishkaaminish-
laaapooortah
186. Kritoulaaapaaakishlaaaneeetou-
laaa
187. Preestolupaaatanaaakriiistoopish
188. Kristolaaaneeeppeetaishmanish
189. Bleeestolaaaamanaaapish-
kreesaatil
190. Tristolaaanooupeekrishtaaala-
naaatooot
191. Chilqulaaanoouraaapeetraan-
ishlatil
192. Strunishkaaateeetobraaaaalaaaa-
titishpaaa
193. Xtruupeeeeloooonishkaaapeeet-
laaamish
194. Tristoooolaaapeetnaquishtraaa-
liinooostupinooootlaaakreeest-
rupishlaaa
195. Stupinooootlaaakreeestrupish-
laaa
196. Skeeporaaalaaanapiirooo-
laaapaaateeet
197. Bristoooopaaleeetraaanishka-
teeeetpatish
198. Kristooolaatooopaaatvaaaaleera-
mish
199. Striiiitkrupeeeetnaaaalaapish
200. Briaallaaatukaaarstreeetnu-
vaaaspaatish
201. Strupeeetlaaakiiishnapishfaaaas-
aaareetmisha
202. Treeeplaaaatkviisaaapishvraaa-
teeeelish
203. Shinuupaaaataalaaaveeepkiiit

204. Princeeepaalaaasiiipootaaaha
205. Krisooootlaaaaariispreetmaala
206. Kloootapeenaaapishlaaakrto-
laaamupaaateeetvarish
207. Priiiteeepaaaalaaariiiishtkrip-
ishnaaa
208. Streeepaaaalaaanaaati-
quaaaleepqva
209. Treeepuuulaaaaafaaataaveee
210. Skreeepaaanaaataaalaaatuupat
211. Kelvanamaaeshvaviishmaoomva
212. Prooostiishpaaanystoolishnaaam
213. Klaaastoolishtaaanoupattish
214. Twiiliishmaaanishtoobeeelaaa-
neeesh
215. Kraaasoooviiitishlaaaamiiniish
216. Tvooolaaanemaaanoooulaas-
toooviish
217. Krepaalanishkaaaapluuyaanish
218. Tellouuprlktooopaaaneeepky-
sish
219. Preeezystishlaaaanoupaaankish
220. Booorlaaashxiiaaaalboortaaash-
niishpaaatanish
221. Kreeeptooolishmaaaniish-
poootaahlish
222. Staaaloooraaah
223. Kiishnaaapooutaalpish
224. Stoohlraaapiilishnaaatoolaapish
225. Oookaaapaaaveshiiiaaamresaa-
abliiioooshraaam
226. Pliiinoooshaaareebaaaheemi-
ishaaakaaploosh
227. Koomuuvaaasaaiiizoovnaape-
shaaaweee

228. Haaluubeeeniioookre-
shaaavoooshuueem
229. Ooomeeshaaalivaaneshaaaoomi-
ishoouur
230. Vaasnoolaaabreeviishakoomeem
231. Raajiibuuraa-
baanesheeemaavaaam
232. Faaaniluumaaooneemishuuraam
233. Bluuiiwaaapreshaaakaaviishaa-
nah
234. Aiiiookaadeve-
shoooriiimaapaadeish
235. Waaalaahiimeeneshaadkaa-
reeem
236. Biiizoooraaveshaaaiimlaaa-
koooraab
237. Saaanaameeshaalaaazeple-
shooraaaiii
238. Teeiiigoraaahi-
imooshaaavaazeeer
239. Kriipkaaatooolaaatiipishkaataah
240. Vaaashmaakaalaaeeiiohmakiive-
naashchiimaankiiin
241. Dooshlaatechiivanaashlaaaoon-
ashkovaniichmaakaaan
242. Vondaashchiiboooeemiiticho-
kaaaanaokaven
243. Liikaaaooiintenviiidaankaano-
maaiichiivoonaashaaki
244. Aahnaaakaavaaaooiinoeeemvi-
ishkaavoohnaashiinchitvaaaash
245. Aashmaaneeshaaveeshaavaaee-
shaambaaeesh
246. Eeaashmuueeshiiaamuuaaee-
shaeeshaaaamaaavooeevaaee-
shaanoom

247. Treeellavaashniishvaamiish-
vaaooeem
248. Pliishpaaraamiishvaroomeesh-
paraam
249. Viishmaaeemaaemblaaaviish-
maaem
250. Saliimaavaashtraeemaaavaaas-
tareem
251. Berelliimaavooshtaeemavam
252. Ooovaamiishvaaoonaaraas-
haaooveraashaanmaakeshlaaraa
253. Oooreshmaaraaookaraanaaoosh-
emkeshlaaraamaaooraaa
254. Maashemkaaraashemkaalesh-
maaraamaakeshmaa
255. Oomaaashevkaaanaashemkev-
naaaoshemshevaaaleshoshem-
raasevkalamaashemvashemraa
256. Ooomaakevshaalaraash-
emkaaveshaamkevshaaraa-
laanashaa
257. Aamaarkaaveshmeeshaameesh-
emraalaashevraakevraameshraaa
258. Aaamaareshkaulaarnaaviish-
naakeshoshemkaalaaraaoooraaa
259. Iishnaaaraamaaalaaknavaraaish-
nakernaavishatooraanesheer-
ashnaaa
260. Vishnaakarnaakeshlaavernaab-
ernaavishnaasheknarashem
261. Viishnakarnaaseshaaaosaashem-
kaaooshaaarshoooraaa
262. Eeshnaravookeravishnookerara-
hoolaanaavishnaaa
263. Meeshemarookesharoomaaesh-
laveeraashemkanaroosh

264. Shemrakemrashemlashemraker-
ashemlaaveeraashooraaa
265. Vishnakaroovishnaroojaaakaraa-
viishiiranurooshaaa
266. Kemleshneshnavoorake-
shraaooraneshkemranooraker
267. Tiloukaaaapeetilishnaaasveet-
baahish
268. Treeeplanishvaaapaaatlaaaput
269. Phaaatdoooraanishplaaatoorta-
anish
270. Restoooulishmaaapishtaaanaqui
271. Lileeepuutnoorapishkaaaliit
272. Trispoouraaanishplishpaaavaaat
273. Ooshmaleshkaalopishmaao-
draashkooshmen
274. Veshiiaaashchiiiholaashmen-
shaaaiioo
275. Pooshiishkaamiischaalaooiish-
meeeooshen
276. Laashchiimenshieenovaalashi-
moraashten
277. Viishtaableneshaanapiiashenko-
shamenaa
278. Voshiintushaankochaanash-
vascheniikaa
279. Aashemashiienaashaavachi-
noshtrashchiimina
280. Indiciiashplaashaeeemishtaaki-
nooravechimen
281. Feliishmaapoochiiiameshache-
niiaeeeolaashenskiish
282. Laashenooaashmaanachiraash-
piichivuteshmiiin
283. Tushpaashiineklashanovash-
chipeeeniia

284. Vulasheeenkoshiipeschchiia-
vaaasheenko
285. Liishaamenchishaaaeenmeeshi-
ivaas
286. Oshnaaashaanaviishooenla-
maaneshotrashovaas
287. Waashemiishkolaaaeeokivashta-
ashenchiooo
288. Miiishaaenooshiiiaentoshiban-
teeeaamo
289. Fiiliishaaeenoshtenushenkash-
vasheniishkooaam
290. Ooooshaamiichaaeeemshaal-
eemvaaashoooeem
291. Vaaaasheemoooeesheenaashii-
meenvaashmaaooeen
292. Viiiishnaashumeeenooshmati-
ishpooaaanem
293. Oolaaashiiteemvaaleessha-
meeniiioon
294. Aaaschvaaneeshijemaamiichi-
pushmaateem
295. Looshvaaaneeshmoshaan-
vaaloooshiimaaooeeen
296. Kiiishmaaneeshkoshaa-
naamoooeenkaamon
297. Maaiishvaaraashiioomvaaeeriim
298. Heeiiaaraabiishliishvaaraash
299. Rooaamaarviishenooruuvaan
300. Keeiishliishfeeshuuraam
301. Vikelaamaadaamuuelvaaraku-
daam
302. Laavaaeeiisheenoomuuaaraa-
teelee
303. Aaaaraaaashmoouuaavaariioosh

304. Biishmaahaashreeiiamo-
     ouueesh
305. Shaanaaraavaaoouushmaraash
306. Kiaavaashaarvaaoomiieereeeesh
307. Goraleenaashaaroom
308. Eeekaarooneeamos
309. Maareeoodoshuruungh
310. Veeoopaaruutchaaruun
311. Sheechaapoorashtailiin
312. Ooomtraachapaaliindraa
313. Woondraashtapogroovdaa
314. Uumbraachoonglaatriimaa
315. Wooshiingroomaalaamooviildaa
316. Maadoowoombeeloodraameen
317. Gooraashtaalaayaamoorashtiim
318. Aarooraashtayiimaaoodra
319. Shtaayaameenooshtaayoom
320. Paanaaavaamiilaatuuuaashaavaa
321. Shiinnaaatraavaaamiil-
     laabraaavaa
322. Kiiwaaauumaaashriinaamaawaa
323. Chaaaliimaaaslishooovnaas
324. Sooeetraauflevaakreemeei-
     ishoopeteshaasaava
325. Buleemaavelkraasheemaavii-
     shba
326. Zuuleemaaviishkaaellaa-
     beemaavaakuum
327. Aamaaaamaalamamuumava-
     laam
328. Metelviishmaaleemavamaaraam
329. Bemelviishmaakretleemaa-
     beemaavuum
330. Haaneshaaveiieeskraaupeshoo-
     bepaataaah
331. Yuubleshaaanooreeejiiwaazoaar

332. Gaaadiieshaaaseiijeemeeshaaket
333. Faaneshyuuoobleemaasaaeloot-
     riel
334. Waaiiedaamooshaaraalooimiing
335. Vaaelaameishaaakooshuuraabi-
     im
336. Bezooliieemaavorshaadekouuni-
     itomaabeen
337. Aaxetooveebulekooshaaveshta-
     ameaalornek
338. Mashraashemraakeraoshemo-
     maaaremshaakershaaoshem
339. Omanshenkashemaaraamaaoo-
     mashenkarshemkaraaamaaa
340. Eemshaneerkaashemoshem-
     raaemshemoshamkevaashem-
     raaa
341. Oomanshenkashemaaraamaaoo-
     mashenkarshemkaraaamaaa
342. Shemaarkeshmaaramaarkesh-
     maareshmaakemlaaashem-
     kaareshmaaa
343. Oooraashemraaookaraa-
     tooooomaaraahjaahaarooshem-
     kaaa
344. Aavechshemkaaavershemkaaas-
     hemaakaavraashemrakavshaaa
345. Triipooliiniishkaaaatalloormish-
     naaapalaatoush
346. Plaatolpiiliishkaaatooliniishtaala
347. Braaatoooulpootalaaanooopiish-
     katooloooorpouliish
348. Kaaataaanupooorinishtaaapilan
349. Staaalaaaniishtiilpoutaaalaan
350. Ooshemkaveeoshemwaooshem-
     veeaashemkaaa

351. Ooooshemwaaviiooshemka-
ooooshemwaaaoooshemkavii-
iaaa

352. Viioooshemwaaaoooooveesh-
naveeoshemkevnaaaoooshem-
waaveenaaa

353. Veeenaashemomshaaaomshava-
meeenaaameenaavoshemkaaas-
hemvanomeeenaaa

354. Meeenaavoshemkaaashem-
kanoveeshmaaaveshmanokev-
naaakevnanoveeshmaaa

355. Keshmaanoveeshmaaaveesh-
maanokevnaaakevanokeeshmaa-
keeshmamokevnaaa

356. Eeemaanookevnaaakevma-
noeeshmaaeeshmaanoveesh-
maaakevmanoeeeshmaaa

357. Eeshmanokevnaaakevma-
noeeshmaaeeshmanokevnaaake-
voshemkevnaaa

358. Ooooshemkeveeenaaaoshemka-
kevnaaaoshemkaveenaaaveena-
ashemooomwaaaoshemkaveeen-
aaa

359. Veeenaaoshemkaaashem-
kaaaooveenaavenaaoshem-
waaashemvanokevnaaa

360. Eeevenasheeemaaasheemaa-
nokeevnaaakevnaaaooshaa-
naaaoshemkaveenaaaveenaosh-
emkaaashemkanoveenaaaveena-
voshemwaaashemkanoveemaaa

361. Veemanokemwaaooshemka-
veenaaaveenaaoshemwaaaosh-
emkaveenaaa

362. Ooooshemwakevnaaaeshme-
nasheewaaashewaanoshem-
kaaaoshemaveeemaaa

363. Eeemanoshemkavashem-
noveemaaaveemaaoshemwaaas-
hemwaanoveemaaa

364. Eeeshmanoshemwaashem-
oshmeshemwaaoshemwavee-
waaaveewaoshemkaaa

365. Oshemwaveemaaaveemaaosh-
emkaaashemwanoveeewaaavee-
waanoshemkaaaa

366. Oshemoveewaaaveewaaosh-
emkaaashemoshemveewaavee-
waoshemkaaa

367. Ooooshemkaveewaaaveewaaosh-
emkaaaoshemwaveewaaavee-
waaoshemkaaa

368. Oshemvaveeenaaveenaoshem-
kaaashemoshemveewaavee-
waoshemkaaa

369. Oshemkaveewaaaveewaaaosh-
emkaaaoshemoveewaaavee-
waaoshemkaaa

370. Priistoooliinkootaaanishpaata

371. Shtooliinkaatuurlaaastupish

372. Fiiiliishoomaaneshkoschaani-
imaaaeeeen

373. Draaashmeeshchnaavoshkiil-
eemvoolem

374. Draaamaasheeniis-
chmaankovaaleesch

375. Swaashmiishaaoooemaashi-
inovaashen

376. Iiimeshaankoeeshiitaahmush-
aaeemiioom

377. Viiishiishlaahmenchiivenushka-
oooemen
378. Kriistooloonpaaakiishtalaliinoti-
ish
379. Trooopiilaaaniishkaaaalaano-
opishlana
380. Tvoolaaanoopiishtraaaniish-
piiishkaala
381. Foortuulaanooopkaaalaaapeeer-
laanoooshtaaap
382. Stooolaanooohlaaaneeepkaatili-
ish
383. Stoorpaaatlooopaaartoouliishta-
apishtish
384. Triintooovaaaatlaaaiipiitiish-
kaaanpa
385. Stiinpooouliiniitiishkeepoout-
laaaniish
386. Xtooolooounooptvooolaaapiil-
ish
387. Kaaliiischemiishaaooohmaa-
maashoovaanaaooeeem
388. Toooshaamiishaankaali-
ishovaaaeeoohmentesh
389. Vlaaaasheenkoomeeniishvaa-
neemoshen
390. Laaashiinaavaasheenkolaahna-
ashmiishenooaam
391. Ooovaaashemraaaoooshaaa-
maaakaaraaameshraaa
392. Shemkaraaaooleshmaaara-
aaloooashkaaaraaamoooe-
shraaakeshraaa
393. Ooomrashaaakeshaaashek-
raaaoshaaaoshaamraashaam-
kaaraaooshaam

394. Eeshraaaoookaareshaaaooo-
kaaaaraaoooshaamke-
shraaaoooshaam
395. Eshraaaoshkaamoshkaam-
reshnaaaoshaamraaas-
haamooooshaamooooshaamraas-
haam
396. Iivicheshnaaacaaarcaaashem-
raaasheshnaaa
397. Eshnaaaveshnaaraaacaaara-
aavaaashemraaakeraaashem-
raaashemkaaa
398. Braavoodraayaandrashtaan-
graangraajemaashraaeemjaay
399. Biishveeriiaashmaavaaraamiish
400. Aammaaniishaaiibi-
ishoonoomaalaaaashmeeniiviio-
omuun

Appendix III: 100 Angels from Andromeda

The following are 100 angels who carried the Andromedan fairies to Earth.

1. Iskaooreempelshnatorvirabim
2. Peleshvreemparvekellesnisator
3. Kreeshbraursetvraneeshbilesva
4. Kreespahurstraveeshspelechna
5. Klisubertraheeselkrauuveesbak-liavet
6. Pooveksaketreshuremvablish
7. Inavishkelesnatorspelechva
8. Vereshplituraveemskatekvaspa
9. Ineshvaturkelesvaspaureempa
10. Klishpanesturpaplishnavech
11. Kelesvareemoonestaurivashka
12. Belesvapaturemvisnestauris
13. Galvaneshuestraveshpelimsa
14. Kelvestrapeshplishvanechsabim
15. Vishmapaooestravechkalim
16. Selvastraneeshuvechsatretvabim
17. Lemueluleemavavechsalim
18. Trekvapelshsakuretva
19. Vetklapelshsakutureemba
20. Kurespareemvareskanetspa
21. Belshvapaturureemvanes
22. Klishvanestaruravatraes
23. Kelimvaneshuempavastrapa
24. Keeshrabutinofvracup
25. Rameetafkabrutinoffvrachin
26. Soocheetofkendorfintoukin
27. Oolemdofbetordinkofra
28. Simoloftokrajindorfkar
29. Beetofdeerofprageeshkarov
30. Velekshabeemuvranecholum
31. Havrabahneekrushpazot
32. Humlareemvazpahkleshnasplev
33. Blishpaataaharishnameerahakut-mintarooha
34. Miraparveksateshhiraparumph-neetaminhatika
35. Vraneeshshubaatpaatelkrik-vaturbareem
36. Shellashutapareemhanakulta
37. Ichtabavuutkreespatachturvit-retorim
38. Tretoreemtravabachvaranesh-kliva
39. Tereshmaheereshstravortrebita
40. Ichnatorbarutshabutkreeshnavut
41. Nuranveetkrelochausnatvikur
42. Luveekraustrebaaslichshneetur
43. Plerechnutstraenlachmitku
44. Semritelleslimumvachoorlu
45. Besvarutbeeslekritnauspa
46. Tirpeesnitkeeslausvinpel
47. Molchanpeeklisveerinstra
48. Nirausfaarechplishpatkees
49. Hefnichshonhoflamprish
50. Keraumpashkleetvrinoch
51. Kremichvaasleempelesvra
52. Virumkaliverimkulech
53. Traufashinpeesamkleesum
54. Norepstrivastulechspi

55.	Krianumetripelkivastranet	78.	Poostrilunkamaleeshtraveel
56.	Nachbinstrovuetvasklaurvit	79.	Ishprotishpauriklaneem
57.	Nechbrishnapuskelitvasbak	80.	Trishnaleemkupirkalim
58.	Rechnotlarchenschneevelspar	81.	Prakeeshtabritalaneem
59.	Kuentiavitkreeheesbaklemp	82.	Strapilishtakiranimpotil
60.	Menhespiklaatvaheeslifparvech	83.	Trilkotlipootoonish
61.	Lachmitkleevithofstrautvra	84.	Krispoortaplttrolanim
62.	Nerbeeslavichvarumkeesplech	85.	Stropalunishbatiktrapil
63.	Nochbinpeleshkriaellesumvira	86.	Frostaleemishnakilpik
64.	Bislechnochvaareetskelichba	87.	Kristalleeshnapeetoralinip
65.	Pruveeklasitvarkleetnochpar	88.	Kriputanatirushbatireeptik
66.	Veesbachpleshpreemnochkees	89.	Pritolameeshkapiratin
67.	Nuramshevabeeshkraumachtor	90.	Treenokishnaperim
68.	Kristolaminteeranim	91.	Pootouranipakristaneem
69.	Pleshtaveerishmanip	92.	Pritorichqvapnasheetura
70.	Stropalinishkatirip	93.	Lipoorishnateemuabils
71.	Brostoliishnatirku	94.	Kritorapoostreemvit
72.	Skrutarrunishbatik	95.	Treepoontuvateeplavit
73.	Krantoolaneemkatir	96.	Chelpootaveepishnatreem
74.	Tropriltokilpeeshkatil	97.	Krostaseemtishnalit
75.	Strepolkutileeshnaptiroklv	98.	Tripolanishtareeptokit
76.	Trinstelishmatreepulapik	99.	Vituraprateelbopirnish
77.	Kqatirulaneekishpatik	100.	Vapreeshtapeetkovit

Appendix IV: 100 Fairies from Andromeda

1. Mechlichshneevasbi
2. Ruvenchlaarshivas
3. Piplechnutvarki
4. Limaumvespreeri
5. Luvechspinoraum
6. Vitlichkreestra
7. Nivamlubeesnich
8. Kaflichnetrabis
9. Vuramspurechmitre
10. Niftrakuuslaavees
11. Neraustruvinsprech
12. Liamvitkreusnochbi
13. Sechlachvitkatrubaas
14. Fleechshatreeauflar
15. Kletklauretnauresbek
16. Hanurekshpek
17. Lauraveksplet
18. Yekslipranuvravechshpipran-auravek
19. Alumanunerunatspi
20. Sitsakruhanerviminskivervinu-halaurael
21. Hispiranukrakulauminel
22. Harapsbinasbitonperek
23. Sitsumehutandrahehu
24. Blisperavunirunonsekrau
25. Kloksumirunelbihenshbititsumi-rael
26. Ararutbelnasut
27. Minuverbiklonklarut
28. Hishtaruatshpemselvi
29. Manuviruhanuvlesbi
30. Ishtanovamirmisu
31. Klanruhavemversabi
32. Vetsparuhapelparvi
33. Hehourvatonparavi
34. Parautravenveshbi
35. Vitruuruaparadoch
36. Letviasturvemsplivech
37. Lautraumiravel
38. Sinsuurubachbeshpel
39. Ratnavaratonumiel
40. Litvamisuravidoch
41. Hanaruhadomverabi
42. Letmiparvichtruavim
43. Launochtrovemparabi
44. Shtanurimruvechvelabi
45. Minirvatruhavimvirsbi
46. Tratrulaunochtrunachshpi
47. Tratrulaunatraunahershpechpli
48. Halahuresbitratulesbimeru
49. Halastemviklaanu
50. Vimvaratklanuversbi
51. Kaatonebismaramu
52. Anotechshbirimuel
53. Tonabelspiunuel
54. Horaletsbi
55. Itsaravunechnesbinu
56. Mananuchshpiminuet
57. Ravasimsuvi
58. Plaaturnamenshbi
59. Horvachtulatraulalu
60. Minshchanatur
61. Lanurichulemlesbi
62. Partalavarunechtel
63. Butnalavech
64. Hirunobinuch
65. Pechspipatelruch

66. Paranovanuvisvi
67. Platernovanurinuch
68. Yesturnabuknasimalatovitutoka-moyamalitakvoronasuitiludehm-enahgoshanamila
69. Enduramojesveetlanashigosha-maniboorlanishiflorahnasibut-toolabokranashiveta
70. Enturalisecondani
71. Miragenilokannavennayeh
72. Ganduramesonapliach
73. Senovapliachmoroda
74. Gennamiodaprelach
75. Coloranashmirodoval
76. Plikasurnasival
77. B?eneraplivahdolamika
78. Enturamiditehsvoyih
79. Yelinasmuyatashi
80. Duramachlainamackay
81. Boormanamelanoma
82. Keeskanarodameeala

83. Kentunamiralanasikoch
84. Enturanashamarila
85. Gondarinisakara
86. Plistacheesnavratushekvon
87. Pluraveeshkavratechniksa
88. Unusheekavrechnabravkar
89. Kauschneevreskrutveechishvan
90. Utraveeshtravechnakvulich
91. Kluskaveechnabrauteknookee
92. Instacheeznavetchibratek
93. Veechplutanekoostrvachkis
94. Strachnakeetelvistravoochneek
95. Ostrookeetelchankavrachtikmek
96. Veenestreeknashvrablevskvool
97. Kleshvooleskivrabelushkiveeka-tel
98. Ostraveeshnagolaumbratschkee
99. Veeshekstraupanichtivenskat
100. Deeshnatechnikvasketvulsime-kvat

Appendix V: The Twelve Pairs of Emotions

Positive Aspect	Negative Aspect

1. Love
The desire to include

Trust
The desire to surrender

2. Inspiration
The desire to be inspired and to inspire

Peace
The desire to be at ease

3. Creativity
The desire to create

Pleasure
The desire to be delighted

4. Empathy
The desire to connect

Acknowledgement
The desire to see the perfection

5. Generosity
The desire to give

Receptivity
The desire to receive

6. Encouragement
The desire to encourage
or to be encouraged

Beauty
The desire to be uplifted

7. Communication
The desire to express

Assimilation
The desire to integrate

8. Passion
The desire to know

Joy
The desire to live

9. Achievement
The desire to excel

Fun
The desire to revel

10. Enlightenment
The desire to enhance or be enhanced

Contentment
The desire to retain

11. Empowerment
The desire to be of service

Humor
The desire to be amused

12. Growth
The desire to expand

Satisfaction
The desire to be fulfilled

The Lemurian Science of Immortality

The first in the Lemurian Sciences Trilogy
The book that will change your life!

Acknowledged as the leading mystic of our time, Almine once again delivers ground-breaking revelations on the art of youthening as translated from *The Lemurian Records of Saradesi – The Fountain of Youth* and *The Tablets of Life and Death*.

As a master translator of records of antiquities, Almine has authored an unforgettable book that shatters existing paradigms perpetuating death.

Windows Into Eternity, 3rd Edition

Revelations of the Mother Goddess
Revised and updated, new images!

This book provides unparalleled insight into ancient mysteries. Almine, an internationally recognized mystic and teacher, reveals the hidden laws of existence. Transcending reason, delivering visionary expansion, this metaphysical masterpiece explores the origins of life as recorded in the Holy Libraries. The release of information from these ancient libraries is a priceless gift to humankind. The illusions found in the building blocks of existence are exposed, as are the purposes of Creation.

Yoga Products by Almine

Irash Satva Yoga
Shrihat Satva Yoga
Saradesi Satva Yoga
Labyrinth of the Moon
The Abundant Life

Irash Satva Yoga

Yoga, as a spiritual and physical discipline has been practiced in many variations by masters and novices for countless years and is universally accepted as one of the most effective development tools ever created. Man's physical form in its original state was meant to be self-purifying, self-regenerating and self-transfiguring. Through pristine living and total surrender, it was possible to open gates in the body that would allow life to permeate and flow through it; indefinitely sustaining it. In IRASH SATVA YOGA, received by Almine from the Angelic Kingdom, this ancient methodology is exponentially expanded and enhanced by incorporating the alchemies of sound and frequency. Using easily mastered postures paired with music from Cosmic Sources created specifically for each, the 144 cardinal gates in the mind and body are opened and cleansed of their dross and debris, allowing the practitioner to tap into the abundance of the One Life.

Shrihat Satva Yoga

The human body is unique in that it is an exact microcosm of the macrocosm of created life. There are 12 points along the right, masculine side of the body and the same number on the left side. These are microcosmic replicas of the macrocosmic cycles of life.

The yoga postures are designed to open and remove the debris from these points – the gates of dreaming. This will occur physically through the postures and the music. Dissolving debris also occurs by way of dreaming (triggered by the breathing and eye movements), releasing past issues that caused the blockages in the points.

Saradesi Satva Yoga
The Yoga of Eternal Youth

As translated by Almine from the ancient texts of Saradesi – The Fountain of Youth

Includes the Sound Elixirs for Eternal Youth
Plus: The Illuminations of the Gods

The ancient texts speak of time as movement. They affirm that time and space, movement and stillness, are illusions. To sustain any illusion requires an enormous amount of resources. This depletion of resources causes aging and decay.

The illusion of polarity, the impossibility that the One Life can be divided and split, is brought to resolution by balancing the opposite poles exactly. Only then can they cancel one another out, revealing an incorruptible reality that lies beyond – the reality of Eternal Youth.

The Abundant Life

By popular demand, the profound words of wisdom that have changed the lives of more than 20,000 daily Twitter followers, communicating in multiple languages, have been compiled into book form. Three hundred aphorisms and mandalas from the Seer Almine will delight and inspire her growing global audience.

Labyrinth of the Moon

The book contains 144 verses of the Poetry of Dreaming and extensive lists of the interpretation of dream symbols. It is a valuable tool for opening up the deeper dream-states' communications, promoting the healing of the psyche, the body and facilitating the balance of the Inner Child and other sub-personalities. Designed to release the hold of past incarnational cycles, it is an essential companion for practitioners of Shrihat and Saradesi Satva Yoga.

CPSIA information can be obtained at www.ICGtesting.com
Printed in the USA
LVOW100359181212

312136LV00001B/4/P